As I Remember: a 1940s childhood

As I Remember

A 1940s Childhood

Gordon Chism

First Limited Edition: October 2004
Second Edition: January 2010

Printed in the U.S.A.

Book Design, Illustration & Production:
Kathy Carl, Avenue Design, Inc.
(cover art created from a photo by Tom Cahill)

Published by:
Avenue Design, Inc.
Fort Bragg, California
kc@avenue-design.com

ISBN 978-0-692-00757-0

*This book may be ordered from your favorite independent bookstore,
online at Amazon.com, or by contacting the publisher.*

Dedicated to the memory of my parents,
John & Mirium Chism

With special thanks to my

Writer's block coach:
Ann Gallagher

Editorial support:
Hilair Chism and Maria Goodwin

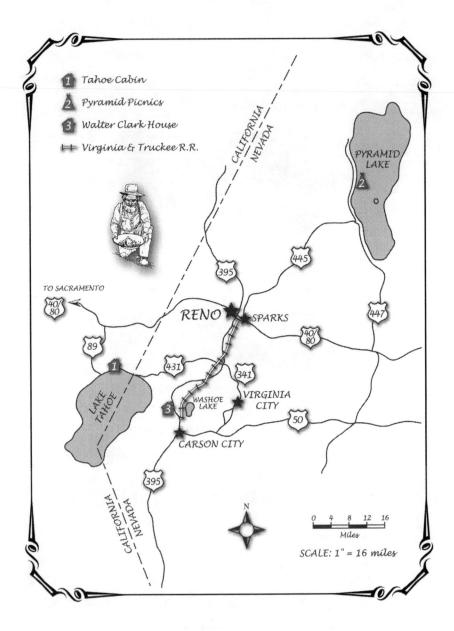

1 Tahoe Cabin
2 Pyramid Picnics
3 Walter Clark House
⊢—⊣ Virginia & Truckee R.R.

CALIFORNIA
NEVADA

PYRAMID
LAKE
2

445

TO SACRAMENTO
40/
80

395

447

89

RENO   SPARKS
40/
80

1

431

341

3   WASHOE
LAKE   VIRGINIA
CITY

LAKE
TAHOE

50

CARSON CITY

395

N

CALIFORNIA
NEVADA

0 4 8 12 16
Miles

SCALE: 1" = 16 miles

Clark/Chism
Home Grounds and Vicinity – Circa 1940s

THE NARRATOR OF THIS REMINISCENCE IS GORDON Chism, the second of four children born to John and Miriam Chism. The predominate setting is the old Chism farm on a gentle bend in the Truckee River at the west end of Reno, Nevada. The period is the early 1940s to the early 1950s. It was an American time of depression, war, and triumph—an exciting journey from economic challenges to nouveau riche.

Possibly the best way to understand this account is through the phrase:

"I am remembering, in ever increasing detail,
*events that I am not quite sure ever happened."**

Origin unknown.

WE BEGIN. I WASN'T AN EASY CHILD ON ACCOUNT of my many allergies. For the first year of my life, I couldn't keep anything down but bananas and I suffered from eczema much of the time. Our family doctor told my parents that it would be easier to make a new one than to keep this one going. Luckily my parents weren't quitters.

The year of 1943 stretches my recall. The radio held the parents' concerned attention with static-laden overseas reports of the war. I had just turned three and had found a screwdriver. I called it my *scewger* and we became inseparable. I took everything apart that had screws—plug plates, door handles, and even my brother Will's crib.

At the very end of 1944, I suffered my first major emotional setback. My father had been drafted. Of course I didn't understand any of it. The bottom line was that the USA was then drafting married men in their thirties with children. My father had a good college friend who worked for Pan American Airways, which had been attached to the military. So with a little help from his friend, my father was able to get around the general draft by taking a job with Pan Am. He ended up on the tiny island of Canton, halfway between Hawaii and Midway.

Somehow I knew my father's leaving wasn't going to be an overnight thing. This upset me greatly. I loved the man. When the taxi came to take my father, I snuck around the adult good-byes and hid on the back seat floor of the taxi. I was going with him. The adults were much amused, but I was in earnest.

My father and me, backyard of our family home – 1942

My mother was now left to manage three children under the age of seven *and* my father's business, Chism's Auto Camp. She was also pregnant. My mother had grit.

I had just turned five and my world was expanding, but not by much since we generally stayed close to home. The war put everything on hold. Gasoline was rationed and my mother was very busy. My sister Betty and I spent a lot of time playing in the fenced front yard or out in the backyard "helping" our mother with the Victory Garden.

The Victory Garden was a wonderland in the summer, with rows of carrots, radishes, and corn. The corn was the largest patch, intriguing and jungle-like. I would crawl into its moist depths where I could see, but not be seen. The raspberry patch brought instant gratification and a freshly pulled carrot could be washed off with the hose for a crunchy treat.

World War II was omnipresent. My mother did the home front thing all the way. Not only did she have a Victory Garden; she was also active in the Red Cross, complete with uniform. We recycled anything metal. I was in charge of peeling the labels off tin cans, using the can opener to cut the bottom out of the can, placing the lid and the bottom inside the can, and then smashing them flat. I was proud to be doing my part.

Behind and to the west of our house, a two-acre vacant lot held a mix of native sagebrush and a neglected apple orchard. About a hundred yards to the north, the war scrap metal dump ran along the railroad tracks. Betty and I spent many days during the war treasure hunting in that dump. I found cast iron piggy banks and pressed metal toy cars. My sister was into old alarm clocks.

From the backyard we could see the railroad tracks. All throughout the war there was a steady stream of trains pulling endless flatcars loaded with olive-drab tanks, trucks, half-tracks, and artillery pieces. Even while inside the house, we knew when another train was headed west out of town because the house began to tremble. At that time, Southern Pacific used the largest steam engines in the world—the massive Malleys.* They had twelve drivers and were so long that the engineer's cab was on the front of the locomotive rather than behind the boiler, allowing the engineer to see where he was going. By the time the train pulled even with our house, the *chug! chug! chug!* of those monster engines, straining to get a hundred-plus loaded railroad cars moving up hill, rattled the windowpanes. You could feel their power through your feet.

Second Street went westward by our house and through the underpass to join Highway 80, then on west to struggle over the Sierra mountains. In those days we lived just outside the city limits on the very western edge of town. There was nothing beyond us but the cemetery and a carpet of sagebrush stretching up to the timberline. By this time, Betty was in the first grade and Will was just two years old, so I had time to myself. About half of the area's funeral processions went right by our house and I hung on the fence and watched the cars go by. I loved the cars.

Mallet Locomotive.

Betty and me – 1944

Funeral processions are now basically a thing of the past, but in 1940s Reno they were a frequent community ritual. About twice a week, the police motorcycles led anywhere from ten to over fifty slow-moving cars with their lights on past our house. Just behind the police motorcycles came the hearse, followed by the limousine (limousines if it was a large funeral) carrying the next of kin. I prided myself in knowing the makes, models, and years of all the cars and would bore to tears any adult who would listen.

With my sister in school, my mother took me with her when she went shopping. Shopping was a frustration because most things were rationed. My mother could buy only about half the meat, butter, and eggs she wanted. She had ration stamps in a book-like folder that was strictly off limits to us children. This was difficult because the stamps were brightly colored, kid-sized, and had cannons and airplanes printed on them. Though often tempted, I never got into them. I could tell my mother was serious.

I was also taken for visits with her mother. My grandmother, Euphemia Clark, was the leader of the pack by the time I came along. She corresponded with and modeled her life after Eleanor Roosevelt. She was bright, stout, liberal, and somewhat imperious. She lived with my grandfather, Walter E. Clark, on Cheney Street about five blocks east of Virginia Street, in a quiet neighborhood of modest but larger-than-average houses. My grandparents' house was medium gray, two-story stucco with a two-arch entry porch covered with grapevines. Off to the right was an outsized willow tree. The house had a large backyard with a double garage on the alley.

Entering the house through its heavy door, I was struck by the quite darkness, the muted tones of the Oriental rugs, and the stiffness of the 1910s furniture. While my mother and my grandmother talked up a storm in the kitchen, I was assigned to play Big Casino with my grandfather Clark. We sat opposite each other at a small table in the front room overlooking the street. I don't remember any conversation, just the playing of cards. Dressed in bathrobe and slippers, he sat in his wingback chair smoking cigars.

Grandfather Clark was an up-by-the-bootstraps nineteenth-century man in the mold of Theodore Roosevelt. As a child in New York, he had been the sole supporter of his mother and aunt; he worked cleaning spittoons. In his teens, he became the manager of an A&P market while going to night school to get his degree. He earned a doctorate in economics and became the chairman of the economics department at City College of New York before he was thirty-five. In 1917, he was offered and accepted the post of president of the tiny University of Nevada. He gathered his new family and moved them from the comfortable eastern seaboard across the country to the Wild West.

My grandfather Clark had an inordinate fear of poverty and invested every penny he could squeeze out of the family budget in the stock market. Before the crash of 1929, his stocks were valued in seven figures.

After the crash, he had a nervous breakdown and never fully recovered.

The place of my earliest memories was our home at 1311 West Second Street. It was a good example of a late thirties two-bedroom one-bath starter home—white with forest green trim, two stories, and two dormers. Three old apple trees graced the front yard, which was surrounded by a white picket fence. It looked like it was straight out of the Disney prop department.

A tour of our house as I remember it between 1943-45 goes something like this. The front door opened into the front room. Off to the left was a brick fireplace with double-hung windows on either side. The back wall

My family home, 1311 West Second Street – 1942

had a good-sized window, flanked on either side with built-in bookcases. The window looked out to the backyard. There were hardwood floors throughout the house, with rag-weave throw rugs adding to the hokey thirties western theme. The sofa was a kind of wagon wheel thing of loose cushions with matching armchair and coffee table. The front room, dining room, and hallway had walls of deep stained knotty pine. My favorite item in the front room was a floor lamp just to the right of the front door. It was a wooden piece fashioned to look like an old butter churn. The kicker was that the two curved doors in the barrel part of the churn opened to reveal a small liquor cabinet.

The rest of the downstairs was composed of my parents' bedroom, the bathroom, the dining room, and the kitchen. The bathroom and kitchen were standard issue for the day—small, cramped, and utilitarian. Across the front room from the fireplace a J-shaped hall led back to the kitchen in the southeast corner of the house. The hall began with a closet on the left, where my parents foolishly tried to hide Christmas presents.

The next door on the left was my parents' bedroom. They had twin beds (as in the movies of the time) against the interior wall. Across the room there were double-hung windows facing the backyard with his and hers dressers on each side. What I liked most in my parents' room was their clothes closet. It was lined in cedar, creating an almost intoxicating place to hide.

Through a door off the end of the hall, a stairway led down into the basement. The basement was unsettling.

It was dark, with concrete walls and open floor joists overhead. The washing machine (one of those white barrel affairs with clothes ringer on top), the slate wash-tubs, and a sump were huddled at the north end. Under the tubs and in the sump were masses of uneven spider webs that we were told to never go near—*black widows*. The only light during the day was provided by a lightwell at the north end. Just to the side of the stairs was the furnace, all ducts and dirty. It was a spooky place.

Back up to the hallway, a stairway on the right led to the second floor of the house. An eight-foot landing separated the east and west rooms. The east room was our children's bedroom and the west an unfinished play-room. The ceiling was open to the rafters and the floor was pine plank. My father had rigged a swing in the middle of the room and Betty and I spent hours playing up there, much to our mother's relief.

To the west of our house, a split-rail fence ran north and south for about one hundred yards along our property line. West of this fence was a four-acre lot that came to a point between the railroad tracks and Second Street. Sitting in the northwest quadrant of this lot was the old Chism farmhouse dating from the 1880s.

My great-grandfather Chism was in his late fifties when he married, so was deceased by the time my father was born. I got the impression he was quite a dynamic man, seeking his fortune in Virginia City during the gold and silver rush. Upon arriving, he noticed that the meat shortage looked to be a better financial prospect then the mining industry. So he traveled to the Sacramento

*My grandfather Cyrus Chism, my father John Chism,
and my great-grandmother Chism – 1916*

area, bought a flock of sheep, and spent the next couple of years herding them around Oregon, returning with nearly a thousand sheep. He was able to demand an outrageous price for them. With his new wealth, he purchased a large working farm at the west end of the Truckee Meadows (later to be called Reno). Thrown into this great Wild West adventure were stories of Indian uprisings and encounters with wild animals.

One day in 1945, we went with friends of my mother to look at the Chism farmhouse. Being wartime, any housing was very hard to find and my mother's friends

Chism Farmhouse, 1401 West Second Street

were desperately in need of a place to live. To a small child the house was big, and once inside I was struck by the height of the ceilings, the dust, and general disarray. It had all the attributes of a western ghost town; made of brick, with dying trees and brush all around. My mother's friends viewed the house and deemed it unlivable, even in desperate times. It was later restored by my great-uncle John Chism and his wife Dorothy and eventually became the home that my parents lived in for over forty years.

My mother believed Betty and I should be exposed to religion. Neither side of the family had strong convictions, so my mother decided on the Sunday school of the Presbyterian Church at Second and Arlington streets (later to be torn down to build a motel). It was all stone and vines with little slit windows. The appointed day arrived and my mother dropped my sister and me off for our first day of Sunday school.

The Sunday school of ten to twelve scrubbed children was held in the basement, presided over by a positive, if somewhat drab, woman in her mid-twenties. We listened to Bible stories, did a little coloring, and had a snack. Things were going okay until the teacher explained the birthday program. If one of us had a birthday in a given week, we were to receive a coloring book and a cupcake. This sounded great to me.

Since I had no idea what the date of my birthday was, I volunteered that particular day as my birthday. I stepped up to the teacher to get my goodies. My poor sister was completely mortified and so embarrassed that she refused to ever go to Sunday school again. That put an end to our religious training.

One summer day, my mother's sister, Euphemia Santini, came to visit with her two boys. James was about eight and Clark around three or four. We got along fine, but my cousins were wild. Betty and I watched with saucer eyes as they screamed, threw things, and refused to obey anyone. This was not the sort of goings-on my mother tolerated. My sister and I knew we would be toast if we ever attempted this type of behavior.

We were kicking a ball around the front yard and James kept referring to it as a *shit*. I believe it was the first time I had heard a child use a swear word—I was in shock. Later that morning we were showing our cousins the upstairs playroom when James produced a book of matches and set the hemp rope of our swing on fire. The rest was all a blur. Screaming, pans of water thrown, and some of the strongest vibes I had ever felt from my mother. To my knowledge our Santini cousins, as children, never set foot in our house again. My aunt Euphemia was academically brilliant, but was over-whelmed by children and housework and never seemed to get a handle on domestic life.

Betty was totally absorbed by paper dolls. We had round-nosed scissors for cutting out the printed paper clothes that went on the cardboard man and woman dolls. There were pages and pages of clothes, but I was only interested in the military uniforms. Outfits for naval officers, army air corps, sailors, and soldiers were all infused with magic.

My mother had a spiffy uniform. Her Red Cross dress was of small blue and white stripes with white cuffs and collar. It had a Red Cross patch on the shoulder and was similar to the army nurse outfit in the paper doll collection. When my mother put it on, we knew that a baby sitter was about to show up and my mother would go off to hand out donuts and coffee to the boys on the troop trains.

One day my uncle, David Clark, arrived on leave. He was just off the train and in full naval uniform, complete with overcoat. Being a doctor, he was a commander and his outfit was up to the rank. He had a white officer's hat with a silver medallion on the front above the shiny black bill; white shirt, black tie, dark blue jacket with gold stripes on the sleeves, and an impressive block of multi-colored campaign ribbons. He was just like the paper doll officer, only better. He let me wear his hat, wrestled with me on the floor, and tickled me until I screamed with joy. I was filled with wonder to think that I was related to such a magnificent figure.

In the spring of 1945, my mother took us to a military fair and bond drive over in Idlewild Park. It was held where the baseball diamonds are today. I was in heaven. There was more military hardware then I had dreamed existed—anti-aircraft guns of different kinds, tanks, machine guns of all kinds, Jeeps, and trucks. The one display that put me over the top was the tail section of a Stuka dive bomber. It was part of a real German airplane—matte forest green with a black swastika on the tail fin. I looked closer and yes, there were bullet holes—Wow! This was a real piece of the monster German war machine from half a world away. There was a confident air to the crowd. Gone were the fearful, anxious vibes I had sensed in the adults huddled around the radio only two years earlier.

On a beautiful sunny day in August the war was over. The church bells rang and rang all day long. My mother was joyful. My sister and I were allowed to jump up and down on the front room sofa and throw cushions about, a definite no-no under ordinary circumstances. The phone never stopped ringing and people came to visit. It was the finest of days.

In September, my brother David was born and the family was up to full strength or would be as soon as my father returned.

My father's return was greatly anticipated. I experienced a hard time when he left. In the past year I had a recurring nightmare. In the dream, I am with my father in a downtown setting surrounded by multi-storied buildings. A machine comes down out of the sky. It takes my father and leaves me screaming and running after it. Evidently I would do the screaming thing for real in the middle of the night and scare my mother stiff.

Shortly after my father left, I found a picture of a butterfly that in my heart of hearts I knew my father would really enjoy. I kept that book, with the page marked to show him when he returned.

At this point my father had been gone for a quarter of my conscious life. I just knew he would love the butterfly picture. The day arrived and we all dressed up and went to the train station to greet my father. It was a sunny day. The huge black steam engine, pulling the dark green Pullman cars, hissed past the station and slowly stopped beyond the platform. I had my book to show my father and my sister was wearing her best dress. It was a real occasion.

There were lots of people, colorful dresses, uniforms, and shouts of greetings. There was my father, or at least I assumed he was my father because my mother was all over him. Yes, he liked my butterfly picture, but he was much more interested in my mother.

He was different. I was different. I just stared at him all the way home. He was my father and I wasn't letting him out of my sight.

THE BIG DEAL IN 1946 WAS THAT THE WAR WAS over. Everyone who was coming home was home. There was a strong sense of pride in knowing America had made the world safe for democracy. Things were about to happen. You could feel it in the air.

The neighborhood was changing and there was an atmosphere of great optimism. The war scrap metal dump next to the tracks was cleaned up and a lumber-planing mill was going in. I was now six years old and would soon begin first grade. With my father home, my world was getting larger because I was generally my father's shadow. We were now a family of six living in a two-bedroom, one-bath house.

The war was over, but things were not back to normal. We didn't take car trips because we couldn't buy tires yet. My father needed galvanized pipe to take care of the deferred maintenance at Chism's Auto Camp. There was a building boom, but no building materials.

Everyone wanted everything they couldn't get during the war, but consumer goods weren't easily available. It was still a time of make-do.

For me, the first grade was the real deal. I had looked forward to going to school, but kindergarten had been like a bicycle with training wheels—not what I had in mind. The kindergarten was in the basement under the east wing and lasted for only a half-day. First grade was not only above ground, but had individual desks with hinged tops just like the upper grades.

My first-grade class at McKinley Park School – 1946

The McKinley Park School building looks much as it did in the forties. It has since been renovated, and the setting is also different than it was in 1946. Across the river, wild sagebrush stretched to the base of Newland Hill. To the west, Idlewild Park was surrounded only by farmers' fields. The school had two giant oak trees in front and no fences around it.

The first, second, and third grades were held on the west side of the school, with the fourth through sixth on the east side. There was an imaginary line running north and south dividing the school into lower grades and upper grades, complete with separate play yards and different recess times.

The play yard for first, second, and third grades had swings, a teeter-totter, and a half-dome-monkey-bar structure. We were little people and the apparatus was to our scale. We all frolicked about, but dreamed of the day when we would be in fourth grade and could play on the east side of the school with all its grown-up equipment; basketball hoops, baseball field, high rings, and horizontal ladder.

Miss Grant was the first-grade teacher. She was ancient, probably in her forties. She ran a tight ship but was kind and fair. My parents had always loved me and generally thought of me as a bright lad. So it came as a shock to me when I wasn't the quickest to learn to read. I fully expected it all to come to me easily, like throwing a ball overhand, riding a bike, or doing a cartwheel. No such luck! I wasn't the class dim bulb, but this reading thing refused to come into focus. Today, I would probably be diagnosed as dyslexic and assigned special classes.

Miss Grant had a reward system. The one who could read the longest without making a mistake was given a miniature. These miniatures were greatly coveted. They were usually little brass pots and pans, kettles and cups made in occupied Japan. I gave it my all, but usually came up short. I think I only got two miniatures for the entire year.

Lunchtime was held in the school auditorium on folding tables. My mother made up our lunch boxes with a sandwich wrapped in wax paper, an apple, banana or orange, and maybe a cookie. We got our milk at school for a nickel.

My sister was now in the third grade so I didn't see her much during school, though we did walk to and from school together. We usually walked with the Miller kids—Jack and Jerry, Joyce, Dale and Gail—two sets of twins with a girl in the middle. The Millers lived about a block east of us on Second Street and made up the bulk of our neighborhood gang. Jack and Jerry were a year older than I. Joyce was in my class and Dale and Gail in pre-school.

We got together after school and walked home. It was a different walk than it would be today. Keystone Avenue was not the cross-town, four-lane artery it is now. Instead it was a two-lane, quiet residential street with little or no traffic. With no bridge over the river, it dead-ended into Riverside Drive. All the brick and frame houses along both sides of the street had large front yards with fruit trees, lawns, and flowers. It was a sleepy residential neighborhood.

When we got home from school we were greeted with, "Take off your school clothes before you go out to play!" My mother looked at our schoolwork and we were off to roller skate. Yes, they were clamp-ons. We were forever losing our skate keys, so my mother tied a length of grocery string in a loop through the key eye so we could hang them around our necks.

There weren't any sidewalks in front of our house—they began in the next block towards town where the Miller kids lived. The sidewalks were plagued with section strips and the tree roots caused some sections to lift, making the going a little tricky. The skates were on the clunky side and tended to come off if radical maneuvers were attempted. We had skinned knees, elbows, and knuckles. My mother was forever giving us Mercurochrome and band-aid patch-ups. That didn't slow us down. In '45 and '46, Betty, the Miller kids, and I covered hundreds of miles skating those two blocks.

From my need to monitor my father's whereabouts I came to know Chism's Auto Camp better and better. Viewed from above, the camp resembled a seven-acre pork chop, with Chism Street being the eastern base and Second Street being the north boundary/long bone. The chop part was outlined by the English Mill Ditch that ran right next to and above the Truckee River, making the southern boundary.

A strip of land about one-hundred-feet wide running the length of Chism Street was leased to the

U.S. government for housing University of Nevada war students. There were about twenty-five slab-sided, navy gray trailers along with a prefab washhouse. It was all planted on gravel—government-issue sterile.

To the west, the boundary of Chism's Auto Camp was marked by a row of elm trees, then a row of six trailer spaces, ending with a tool shed. Beyond the student trailers westward was the park. South from the back of the park was a U-shaped cluster of weekly cabins, with a bathhouse and laundry situated at the southern leg of the U.

Behind the laundry, running along the back of the weekly cabins were the clotheslines—no dryers in those days. Backyard clotheslines were a colorful feature of every house. The rest was taken up with clusters of trailer spaces; more like a patchwork quilt than a grid. The newest part of the camp was the eight-unit motel, filling the western tip of the property along Second Street.

At the main entrance to the auto camp, an office building housed a mini-market, the living quarters for the hired couple, a gas station, and the motel office—all in a twenty-four by twenty-four-foot structure. Things were tight. As you entered though the office door, you could see a gray marble counter running through the middle of the room. To the left, a large wooden glass-doored icebox containing milk, butter, and eggs sat along the east wall. Every remaining square foot of wall space was devoted to wooden shelves for canned goods. There was an impressive cast brass cash register that rang a bell when opened.

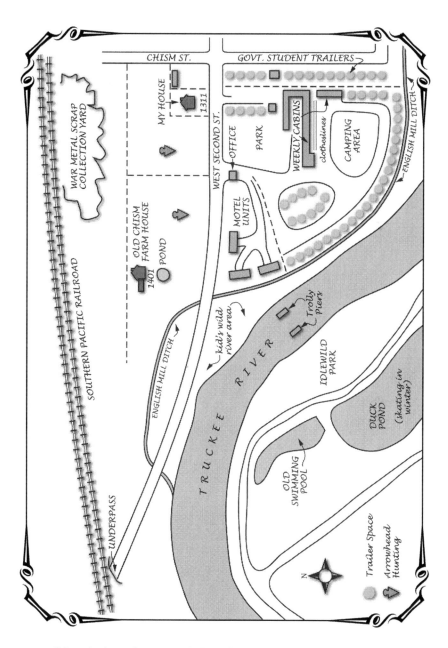

Chism's Auto Camp and Family Neighborhood – Circa 1945

Behind the marble counter on the right was the door to the manager's quarters. This space included a twelve-by-twelve-foot living room to the north street side, a tiny kitchen in the middle, a tiny bathroom behind the mini-store, and a tiny bedroom at the back. My parents lived in these quarters for the first couple of years they were married.

This combined office/mini-store/manager's quarters was essentially the same building as it is today. On the Second Street side there was a canopy over two gas pumps. Above the overhang was a classic thirties neon sign—baked-on blue and white enamel announcing: *Chism's Auto Camp.* Along the western side of the building there was a hefty wooden ramp for cars needing an oil change.

Chism's Auto Camp entrance from Second Street

Just to the east of the office, the road sloped down about three feet. This drop-off created a half-story basement at the back of the office. Today it is dead storage, but in '46 it held the motel's linen, cleaning supplies, and dirty laundry dump—a hub of activity.

All the roads in the auto camp were oiled gravel—not a square foot of pavement. Once you passed the office, the road split. The road to the motel units curved around the office then due west. The other fork went straight back into the heart of the camp.

The tree-studded park with its well-kept lawns was a little more than twice as big as it is today. It went from Second Street about fifty yards deep to include the area occupied by the present bathhouse. The park was bordered by hundreds of one-foot-sized rocks along the gravel road. Where the bathhouse now sits there used to be a couple of wooden picnic tables. The adults gathered there to gossip while the children played at the street end of the park.

About eight to ten children in the five- to ten-year range lived in the auto camp and played in the park almost every day. In the summer, we kids would run barefoot in the moist grass, playing tag and jumping through the sprinklers. When the day was really hot, we begged ice chips from the iceman at the back of his truck. All the campers and trailers used block ice. The Union Ice truck came every other day. If ice was needed, you put a green card in your window.

The park was the last remnant of the Chism farm apple orchard. Almost all of the trees were ancient apple and about four large ones had thick, low hanging branches, creating a tree climber's delight. At night we played hide-and-seek and kick-the-can. When we couldn't find everybody or the game was over we would call out, "Olly, olly, oxen-free!" to reassemble the troops in the park. No, none of us knew or cared what the real words were.

One day, a girl in our group offered to show me and another boy her mysteries if we would give her a peek at ours. This sounded good to me. We went behind the drying-yard fence and were just starting our comparative anatomy lesson when a booming voice snarled, "*What do you think you are doing?*"

I wheeled around only to come face-to-face with hate and anger. I froze. What had happened? The girl's angry father pulled her by the arm in the direction of their trailer. He turned, locked eyes with mine, and hissed, "I am going to tell your father!"

We must have broken a very strong tribal taboo, judging by the father's response, but what it was, I could only guess. The whole subject was shrouded in mystery and secrecy. I brooded over this for a day. I knew I would have to face my father with this terrible transgression of mine. The next day while we were walking together, I broached the subject. I was expecting disapproval and rejection so I was far from eloquent. Through my stammering I was able to get the whole story out. I looked up at my father hoping for mercy. He had a big grin on his face and began to chuckle. I could tell he was stifling a laugh. What was going on?

As previously mentioned, a cluster of weekly cabins was located at the very center of Chism's Auto Camp. These little gems had a bedroom with a kitchenette, and a shower/toilet combo at the back. All this was packaged into a twelve-by-twenty-foot floor plan and rented for eight dollars a week. To say that the turnover was brisk would be an understatement. The clientele tended to be on the colorful side.

There were sixteen of these cabins with five of them in a row running north to south right up against the government student housing trailers. There were two rows that ran east to west, coming off the north-south row, and making a sort of U-shaped courtyard. Each row had a continuous roofline with a cabin, then an open-faced garage, cabin, garage, etc.

Eight-Dollar-A-Week Cabins

The east-west row to the south had the men and women's washrooms for campers and caravans, with the laundry on its west end. The washrooms had concrete floors, a row of washbasins with brass hose bibs off exposed pipes, and a row of open-faced showers. It looked much like a World War II army latrine movie set. The laundry filled the southern half of the western end of the building and was about fourteen-by-twenty feet with slate washtubs along the north wall and two or three of those old tub and ringer washing machines.

One of my earliest memories of the washhouse was the 1946 Halloween party for the kids who lived in the auto camp. We were all in our costumes, bobbed for apples, and had a roaring good time. The auto camp was made up of two separate groups. The eight-dollar-a-week cabin people tended to be an odd bunch and kept to themselves, but the trailer owners formed a real community, alive with characters, gossip, and cliques.

The English Mill Ditch was diverted off the Truckee River about three hundred yards upstream near the railroad tracks. It then wound under Second Street near the underpass parallel to the street, then back under the street again heading south to make a sweeping turn to the east. The ditch formed the western and southern borders of the auto camp.

The ditch itself was about seven feet wide and three feet deep, well-maintained, and flowing year-round. The English Mill Ditch was part of an old series of irrigation ditches that made farming possible in the area. Water rights were still a topic of adult conversation.

Towards the river from the English Mill Ditch, a strip of wild territory about twenty yards deep ran along the river—at least it seemed to be the wilds to a six-year-old boy. This was Huckleberry Fin country with willow thickets, brush, and trees of many varieties. The ditch, a storm drain, and the river created pirate coves and hideouts. As kids we couldn't resist this place.

The river divided the town nearly in two, both physically and socially. The government buildings, post office, courthouse, and library were situated on the south side of the river, with the bulk of the commercial buildings on the north. Virginia Street bisected the town as Route 395 going north and south. The post office was located at the north-south divide, as well as at the east-west divide.

In those days the post office had low hedges and a large lawn that spread to the river. It was lovely then, but now it is all a parking lot. Reno had a population of about 35,000 back then and only about half the people had cars, so parking was never a real problem. One of my favorite activities was to go with my father to retrieve the auto camp mail. This was a daily ritual that commenced about ten in the morning and took about an hour to complete. We got into our car (a black '36 Ford coupe) with the mail sack and headed for town. We usually parked somewhere on the Virginia Street bridge and walked to the post office.

When we approached the steps of the post office someone usually called out, "*John*"*!* While my father talked to this first man, they would inevitably be joined by a second, then a third. They talked over current tidbits, laughed, and then said they had to get going. We got about to the middle of the steps and the scene, with a new cast, would repeat, then occur again inside the post office. These men knew me as Little John and I was proud of it. It was the village tribesmen gathering near the river to pass on the latest news.

In 1946, I wanted to grow up to be a P-51 pilot. I loved those Mustangs. They were the fastest, deadliest planes in the struggle to save the civilized world—they were also beautiful. The Nevada Air National Guard was outfitted with P-51s and the pilots were hotshots just back from the war. Since we were on the very edge of town they would buzz us, flying only about five-hundred feet off the ground. My sister and I would be out in the yard and we could hear that distinctive growling moan, only to look up into an empty sky. The plane wasn't where we looked because it was out-running its sound by a quarter of a mile. As soon as we made the proper adjustment, there it was with the sun flashing off its silver skin. We waved at the pilot and if we were lucky, he waved back. I couldn't help but think that in all that magnificence—power, speed, and sculptural purity—surely the secrets of life must reside.

In the summer of 1946, Colonel and Mrs. E. D. Reynolds, their three children, and their Filipino houseboy visited us. Colonel Reynolds had commanded a wing of B-29's in the Pacific Theatre. He was a pleasant enough fellow, but definitely right of center. The Reynolds were college friends of my parents and had just returned from the Philippines.

Their arrival couldn't have impressed me more. They drove up in an army Jeep and an army weapons carrier, all olive-drab with white stars on the sides and army serial numbers and markings—Wow! I, like all my boyhood friends, was a military junkie and this was too good to be true; real army vehicles parked alongside my house. I could sit in them, move all the controls, smell the military smells, and dream dreams of glory—cool.

Their two daughters were about the same age as my sister and I. Their son, Charles, was closer to my brother Will's age so we all matched up well. The Reynolds children had been raised under a southern influence and talked with a charming drawl. Frankie, their houseboy,

Will, Betty, David, and me – 1946

was in his early twenties, soft-spoken, and obviously intelligent. While the adults caught up on five lost years, Frankie fed and cared for us children. One morning while eating his breakfast, Little Charles called out in a demanding tone, "More grits, Frankie!" It cracked us up. The Reynolds children didn't get it, but to us, the ordering about of an adult by a three-year-old child was absurd. From then on it became one of our family's humorous phrases. Whenever one of us got uppity, someone called out, "More grits, Frankie!"

We had just gotten to know each other when it was decided we would all go fishing at Webber Lake, a small lake to the north of Truckee about halfway up the Sierras. We went in convoy. I asked for and received permission to ride in the weapons carrier. I was in heaven—the canvas top, the open sides, and the hiss of the military tires on the road—this was the real thing.

The last few miles to the lake was a dirt road winding to the north end of the lake. There stood an old two-story lumberjack boarding house with about a dozen rooms. I was delighted to learn that the parents had permission to use the whole place—we had the run of it. It was a ghost-town-like structure, in decay, but serviceable. It had no electricity or running water and the toilets were outhouses. The men went fishing. The women set up the kitchen. We kids explored the woods and the lakeshore. We were happy as dogs at the beach.

We spent about a week in this Wild West adventure, which was the high point of 1946 for me. Colonel Reynolds gave us a set of 8x10 glossy photos of B-29's dropping bombs over Japan. A photographer with an artistic eye had taken them—contrasts of cloud, silver aircraft, and deep shadows. They were great, especially to a dreamy six-year-old.

I overheard my mother telling Colonel Reynolds that he shouldn't expect Frankie to spend his life looking after his children. The colonel replied, "He makes five times what he could make teaching school back in the Philippines—he will stay with me forever." About a year later my mother was delighted to hear that Frankie had left the colonel and was attending a university.

The winters in the forties were much colder than they are today. Snow was a two- or three-month ordeal. It was certain to be a foot or more deep at least three times a season. The house had to be readied: foundation vents covered, yard water shut off and drained, and outside hose bibs insulated. My mother put flannel sheets on our beds. There was usually frost on the windows when we went down to breakfast.

Ice-skating season began in late November and continued through February. Ice-skating parties were held at Idlewild Park every night through the Christmas season. We could see the fires across the river flickering through the trees.

My father was a very good skater. He told of ice-skating on the Truckee River when he was young to work up an appetite for Thanksgiving dinner. In his day, the river froze over every year and everyone skated. Not only could he execute perfect figure eights, but he could also do a trick called the *grapevine* that impressed me no end.

In the winter of 1946, my parents took my sister and me skating at the park. My father and mother had spiffy lace-up figure skates, but Betty and I used hand-me-down clamp-on skates, much the same as clamp-on roller skates. They were socially embarrassing and hell to skate on. It became a standard plea at Christmas to ask for figure skates.

NINETEEN FORTY-SEVEN WAS A YEAR OF CHANGE. The old Chism farmhouse next door was being enlarged and renovated by my father's uncle John and his wife Dorothy. The government student trailers were being moved out. In their place, my father put in new trailer spaces. Our family home was being enlarged. Consumer goods were coming back with a rush and the air was filled with a national confidence.

My uncle, Walter Van Tilburg Clark, his wife Barbara, and their two children had moved into an old ranch house in Washoe Valley. Uncle Walter was a successful novelist and a sort of intellectual Marlboro man—tall, rugged, and handsome, yet sensitive. Aunt Barbara was brilliant, small-boned with a bird-like demeanor. Their children, Babs and Bobby, were my favorite cousins.

My uncle, David Clark, and his wife Marge were back in town and living in a duplex near the Veterans

Hospital. He had a new '47 Chevrolet fastback and was using his G.I. bill to take flying lessons. This really impressed and excited me. Uncle David was my childhood action hero; he had boundless energy and a big smile. Aunt Marge was easygoing and open-minded.

The family was gathering around and there was a warm feeling of belonging. One of our family rituals was the birthday measuring—a much anticipated part of every

Me and Betty with Uncle David, washing his new car

child's special day. The growth chart of the Chism, Clark, and Santini children was recorded on the doorjamb between our grandmother's kitchen and her sun porch.

About mid-morning on your birthday, you would put your back against the doorjamb and stand as straight and as tall as you possibly could, amid charges from the other children that you were lifting out of your shoes. At this point, our grandfather Clark approached in his bathrobe and slippers with an empty cigar box in his left hand and a pencil in his right. He placed the cigar box on your head and against the doorjamb, drew a line across the jamb, and entered the date and your name under your new line.

Then came the exciting part. Our grandfather measured the distance between last year's line and this year's line. He would then award us with a silver dollar for each inch or part of an inch that we had grown. This was our biggest cash payday of the year—two, three, possibly four silver dollars at one time. The silver dollars were beautiful, heavy, and rang like a bell if dropped on a hard surface. They were the essence of hard currency.

Our house, the auto camp, and our great uncle's house next door were all built on land that had originally been an old Indian campground. Indians had been living there on the bend of the river for hundreds of years. My parents showed my sister and me that if we studied the ground carefully in the vacant lot next to our house, we could find arrowheads.

Once our eyes were trained to pick out the flint and obsidian from the other stones, we could see Indian relics everywhere. Mostly we would find broken arrowheads, but we didn't even bother to pick those up. With a little concentration we could find two, maybe three complete arrowheads in just an hour of looking. Betty and I were getting good at this, and in no time at all we had built an impressive family collection.

We were so diligent that easy pickings soon filled our collection and we started looking for new possibilities. We found that the searching was just as good over the split-rail fence to the west on our great uncle's land. We were just getting into these virgin lands when large trucks began dumping loads of topsoil all over our hunting grounds. All of the land between the old Chism farmhouse and West Second Street was to become lawn with a sweeping driveway, and the fill dirt would bring the whole area above street level. We worked hard to beat the trucks, but it was not meant to be. We managed to find some very good pieces, but within a month the site was covered with fill dirt and lost forever.

The Chism's Auto Camp mini-store and the gas station were scrapped and the office was now just an office with the manager's quarters. My great uncle's house next door was also being transformed. Our family home was being expanded eight feet to the east end, with the addition of a bay window in the dining room, and a second bathroom upstairs. I was trying to get a handle on life but it kept changing on me.

I was not only confused by these local changes, but I was becoming alarmed at the major changes that kept crowding into my perfect world. We were now seeing

P-80 jets in the skies. I was still madly in love with the prop driven P-51 Mustangs. It was only a matter of time before the Mustangs flew no more. I was also in love with steam locomotives. In the summer of '47, the first diesel engines showed up and by the end of the year most of the steam engines had been retired. I was always fascinated with automobiles. My real love was the Model A Ford. It was pure of line and function with no unnecessary embellishments, while the new cars were all glitz and short on content. I was in search of stability and all I could see was change.

We kids still had our Huck Finn stretch of river-bank and spent a lot of time playing there. We didn't know it at the time, but we grew up during one of the most severe droughts the area had ever known. The river flowed at only half the level it does today. We could jump from rock to rock and get to Idlewild Park without getting wet.

Prominent in the river where we played were two concrete piers equally spaced between the banks. The piers measured about eight feet tall by twelve feet wide by four feet thick. They had been the first step in the construction of a bridge for a trolley line intended to transport people from downtown Reno to Idlewild Park, but the depression had killed the project. To us they were castle ruins and gave our part of the river substance.

Crawdad hunting was our chief occupation at the river. These mini-lobsters varied in size up to about nine inches and every third rock in the river had one under it. The trick was to grab the body just behind the claws or you got nailed. A big one could really get your attention. In the English Mill Ditch, deep-water fishing was required to catch a crawdad. We tied a piece of bacon fat to a rock with grocery string and let it sink to the bottom in a clear patch of stream. Within a minute, you could see little white specks start to move toward the bacon. The white specks were at the base of the pincers, while the bulk of a crawdad was so well camouflaged that you had to strain to see it in two feet of water. Once the crawdad got hold of the bacon, if you pulled the string up slowly, he wouldn't let go and you had him.

We were also into building forts, playing war, and being explorers. The river was brimming with materials, sites, and inspiration. We were usually so engrossed in our river projects that time would melt away. Then someone would say, "Oh, gee, is it six o'clock?" We had to be home for dinner by then or we were in deep trouble with Mom. Mom didn't accept any excuses.

Dinner at our house was a family gathering and time for sharing information. It had its understood rules. Rule Number 1: everyone had to be home, washed up, and ready for dinner by six. Rule Number 2: no commercial boxes, bottles, or cans could ever be on the dinner table. Rule Number 3: you must follow standard table manners to the best of your abilities. Everyone was listened to and everyone was expected to contribute.

The time after dinner was filled with options. Some nights we would go for a drive. In 1947, the family car was the aforementioned '36 Ford business coupe. My father had taken out the standard shelf behind the seat and built a wooden bench for my sister Betty, my brother Will, and me to sit on. My brother David sat on my mother's lap. We drove through town, checked out the progress on the new Mapes Hotel, and looked at the neon signs. My favorite after-dinner drive was a trip to the airport.

The airport was just beyond the southeast corner of town on Airport Road. As you approached the airport compound, you could see a chain-link fence to your left. Beyond the fence was the tie-down area for about twenty light aircraft leading up to the private hangar that could hold about six airplanes. The Joe Williams Flight School (where my Uncle David was taking lessons) was held in a hundred-foot string of prefab metal buildings that ran along Airport Road, then merged with a larger hangar that housed the tower and the United Airlines terminal.

The United Airlines terminal was a small room with a counter, a vinyl-covered sofa, and a slot machine. To the south of the terminal complex, a gravel parking lot held twenty cars max. This was our after-dinner destination. Our father parked the car facing the north-south runway where we waited for the action to start.

The two-engine DC-3 was the big mover. Tastefully dressed in United Airlines dark blue and white markings, the polished silver monster would accept passengers on the concrete apron in front of the hangar/tower. The passengers walked out the back door of the reception area, down the steps, and out to the DC-3. Since the DC-3 was a tail dragger, it required only a four- or five-step boarding ladder.

With everyone aboard and the plane buttoned up, the two engines were started one at a time. There was a loud whining sound, a cough or two, and the engine burst to life with much white smoke, bluster, and flashing blades. Once the engines were turning over smoothly the great ship would start to roll, idling past us and on down to the south end of the runway, a half-mile distant.

We could hardly hear or see the plane at this point. Then a deep roar would start to build and we could see it begin to move. By the time the plane was even with us, the tail was up and the roar was so powerful that we were enveloped in its splendor. As it passed us, the Doppler shift lowered the tone. The silver monster was up and on its way to, I was sure, great adventures.

Another after-dinner entertainment was listening to the radio. My father had purchased and assembled a Heath Kit radio; it was then a do-it-yourself way to a better radio. He built it into the bookshelves on the north wall of the front room. It worked well, but I couldn't detect any great advance over the old radio.

The whole family was engrossed in *The Whistler*, *The Shadow*, *The Jack Benny Show*, *Allen's Alley*, *The Bob Hope Show*, *Amos and Andy*, and *Fibber Magee and Molly*. Every week featured an adaptation of a literary work— *Tale of Two Cities*, *The Count of Monte Cristo*, etc., with current movie stars in the title roles. Yes, it was the theater of the mind, but even more, it was a primal gathering of family around the hearth to hear tales. It's difficult to explain now, but back then we all believed everyone in the family was in mental accord. We felt we were on the same page creating all of this together.

Nine o'clock was bedtime for us kids—it was non-negotiable. That's when under-the-covers reading of comic books by flashlight or, in my case, unauthorized radio usage, took over. For years I followed the intrepid daring-do of Reggie and Jack in *I Love an Adventure*. The program was only fifteen minutes long, but oh, what a rush! I don't think I could have taken more than fifteen minutes. At ten o'clock every weeknight the duo explored lost worlds in the Amazon jungle hidden by rock cliffs thousands of feet high. They encountered half-man, half-beast, hairy club-wielding creatures that wanted Reggie and Jack's beautiful female companion. Modern special effects can't compare with the scenes that radio created in my mind.

My favorite Saturday morning kid's program was *Big John and Sparky*. It started off with a deep voice proclaiming, "Plunk your magic twanger, Froggy!" which was followed by the comic sound of a spring being released. Even in those days most of the kiddie programs were scary. Tales of evil Arab sheiks, gunfights, and giant spiders were the usual fare. I also followed *Red Ryder*, *Hopalong Cassidy*, *Superman*, *Roy Rogers*, and *Sky King*.

One day my father announced that the circus was in town. We all piled into the car and drove to the railway siding to have a look. It was the combined Barnum & Bailey-Ringling Brothers Circus unloading about twenty silver-painted railroad cars. Elephants were an amazement to me—elephants and the general excitement that swirled around the mystique of the circus. But I could sense that this was no longer the hey-day of the circus. The railroad cars needed new paint and their equipment was a little on the needs-an-overhaul side, but the spirit was still there.

Yes, we were going to the circus on a beautiful summer evening. A large vacant lot across from the rodeo grounds was the site, and so many other people were going that we had to park about two blocks away. Unbelievably large tents were erected, creating a tent city with a smell that got stronger as we got closer. It was a barnyard-like smell, only deeper and richer. That night was my first taste of cotton candy and the push and shove of the crowd. My favorite act was the aerialists. Swinging high above the crowd and leaving one swing hanging in mid-air, then catching another, thrilled me. The kids in the act were hardly older than I, which surprised and delighted me.

The animal acts were certainly exotic, but I felt that the animals were not really enjoying the whole process. In between the major acts, the clowns performed. They were fun to watch, but the miniature clown cars fascinated me the most. I was sure I could make my own clown car if I could only get the parts I needed. I was anxious to get home and start designing.

I was glad to finally have first-hand knowledge of the circus. The circus was often mentioned in children's books that my parents read to us. While the whole outing added to my personal experience, I certainly felt no pull to leave home and join the circus.

Our mother was trying to encourage us kids to be responsible for our surroundings and ourselves. She drew a graph for each of us with the days of the week along the top and a list of daily duties down the side: make our bed, brush our teeth, pick up our clothes, help with the dishes. The lines across the chart under each duty formed a box, with lines coming down the chart dividing the days of the week. Our charts were posted on our bedroom wall for all to see. If we did a great job at a particular task we would get a lick-&-stick gold star; an okay job earned a silver star, and a red for a not so good. Betty was a gold-star demon. Will and I had more color variety. If we did a passable job for the week, we received an allowance of twenty-five cents.

Ever since my sister started school, all of us seemed to end up with measles, mumps, colds, and viruses at some time or another. When we were sick, my mother took really good care of us. We got to be in one of our parent's beds downstairs and were served meals in bed. The doctor came to our house with his black leather bag. He listened with his stethoscope, took our temperature, and told my mother how to handle the situation. She doted on the sick child so well that the rest of us would accuse the sick one of faking just for the attention.

Around our house, building things was a primary pastime. Chism's Auto Camp purchased toilet paper in case lots that came in large cardboard boxes. My father brought these boxes home to us kids. We made ships, planes, cars, and trucks by cutting out windows and doors with a bread knife, then filling in the appropriate markings with crayons. The new planing mill behind our house was a great source for building materials. Will and I were still struggling with the mastery of the hammer and saw, causing many black thumbnails and saw rashes, but build we did.

My father built a six-foot-high fence around our backyard, which proved to be a good base for our forts in the adjacent vacant lot. Will, though very young at the time, was a born builder. The two of us always had a building project under way. We built a three-story fort against the fence. We built an airplane and hung it in

My mother, me, David, Will, and Betty – 1947

the apple tree in the front yard and we had numerous wooden car projects.

Our parents were more than tolerant of our efforts. They came out to see what new part of the yard we were reconfiguring and to give us encouragement. I believe we got this building knack from my mother who always had a craft project in the works. In '47 my mother made dolls with plaster heads and pipe cleaner bodies. She then sewed outfits for each, and cast plates and cups with hand-painted designs for their table. We thought this was really cool.

Every year a troop of Gypsies camped down at the river and made lawn furniture out of the willows, which they then sold door-to-door. My mother was a customer. The Gypsies were very exotic creatures, like people out of a fairy tale—dark and mysterious.

My mother had more energy than the rest of the family put together. Along with her doll house projects, she took down the west side of the front yard picket fence and started expanding the lawn westward along Second Street, making our front yard two hundred feet wide. At the same time she and my father put in chicken pens just to the west of the house.

I think the chickens were an attempt to save enough from the family food budget to help pay for the addition to our house. It was a disaster. With expensive feed we were able to raise about two dozen chickens that summer. They proved to be athletic, aggressive, and smelly. My mother made my father do the killing. Luckily we weren't involved in that, but we did participate in the feather plucking. My mother only cooked about half of them. They proved so tough and stringy we could hardly eat them. We all tried to put a brave face on the project, but chicken farmers we were not.

My mother, and everyone else's mother, ironed for hours every day. Everything was ironed—sheets, pillowcases, napkins, tablecloths, shirts, pants, dresses, handkerchiefs, etc. If it was made of fabric it was ironed. With the new addition to the house, my mother had a laundry room—a place to iron and listen to the radio. Swing music became the background of my childhood and to this day I get a feeling of well-being whenever I hear it.

The addition to the house included an upstairs bathroom in the kid's dormitory. We all slept in the same room, with three beds against the north wall and our brother David's crib in the dormer. It was at this time that our parents put a lock on their bedroom door. We couldn't figure that one out.

My brother Will had a habit, while fast asleep, of getting on all fours on his bed and pounding his head into the wall in a continuous rhythm. My mother put a pad on the wall so he wouldn't make so much noise. His sleepwalking could be even more dramatic. One morning we got up and Will was gone. We looked all over the house and my father ran out to search the neighborhood. He was found in his pajamas walking toward town along the railroad tracks.

My mother took her job seriously. She was a driven woman and her profession was wife and mother. She was going to be the best mother ever, and I have to say she was right in there. She was determined that her children be exposed to the better things in life. A trip to San Francisco, now that Betty was nine and I was seven, seemed appropriate. Our two brothers were to stay home with a baby sitter. Since the family car wasn't up to the task, we went on the train, much to my delight.

The train was wonderful. We were in our best clothes—train travel and San Francisco demanded it in 1947. I had on a suit and tie and felt constrained and a little self-conscious, but I knew that I was being included in an adult mission. I tried to look natural. As we boarded, I came face to face with the first black man I had ever met. All the porters and dining car waiters were black. They seemed to sense that I was in uncharted waters. They accepted and welcomed me—I felt we were friends.

The dining car was the best restaurant I had ever experienced. All the tables had white tablecloths, crystal, two forks, two spoons, and a vase of flowers. All the men were in suit and tie and the women wore dress suits. I felt like I was in a Fred Astaire movie. Not only was it a fine restaurant, but we were flying along through the mountain forest as well. It was almost too much for a river rat like me.

I probably fell asleep at some point since I can't remember much of the Sacramento part of the trip. But as we neared San Francisco, I was entranced. There were marshlands, channels with small boats, and mysterious buildings with docks—scenes I had only witnessed in *Captain America* serials where the bad guys holed up. I was living an adventure and we were not even in San Francisco yet!

Once in San Francisco, I was all wide-eyed and open-mouthed. Even the air was different. It was so soft, moist, and exotic. I had never experienced the damp feel or the smell of the ocean air. We stayed at a hotel that was the largest building I had ever seen. The whole scale of the city was super-sized. It wasn't just twenty times as big as Reno, it had wonders Reno couldn't dream of. There were twenty-story buildings, streetcars, and hundreds of taxis; steep hills with cable cars, the bay, the bridges, the big-time hustle and bustle. I was becoming a man of the world and it was only my first day.

Walking the streets felt like being in a movie. Most of the women were in dress suits, hats, and gloves. The men, with few exceptions, wore dark suits and ties. The pace was swift and all business. I, on more than one occasion, had to be snatched from the path of taxis and streetcars. I couldn't stop gazing at the tall buildings and the neon signs.

Both my parents had spent time in San Francisco and were out to show us the sights. We took a colorful streetcar out to the zoo. It was the old-style upright streetcar with panel sides and overhanging roof. It was a pretty good trip with at least one transfer. I was amazed at the row houses, each a tiny palace with a theme done in stucco details—columns, porticos, arched windows, and elaborate staircases.

As we arrived at the zoo, I was once again hit with that aroma of the ocean, only stronger this time, since the zoo was next to the beach on the ocean side of the city. My father got our tickets and we were off to investigate the exciting sounds drifting up to us from the interior of the zoo. We heard the screeches, barks, and roars—the calls of the wild.

There were incredible birds, primates, elephants, and cats in such profusion that I couldn't keep up. My mother checked on the feeding time for the lions as my father took us to Monkey Island. This was one of my favorites, with at least fifty monkeys living wild on this huge rock formation surrounded by about thirty feet of water. The seal show was a hoot and the bird aviary was a real jungle experience.

My mother rejoined us with news that the feeding was about to begin. The same dress code seemed to apply even at the zoo. We, and the majority of others, were in suits—weird. I also noticed the unmistakable sound of a steam whistle coming from someplace nearby.

The feeding of the lions took place indoors. An impressive concrete building, over a hundred feet long with ceilings at least twenty feet tall, was solely dedicated to this ritual. It was initially quiet. The crowd of about thirty zoo-goers was milling about and looking into the barred cages that spanned the south wall. Then the metallic clank of cage doors was heard and the guttural rumble of great beasts filled the space.

There they were, far larger than I expected. The air was heavy with primal excitement. The great cats were tense and roared and threatened the cats in the adjacent cages. Large quantities of raw meat on the end of steel poles were being passed through the bars by the zoo staff. When the lions got their meat, they snarled and grabbed it with claws and bit it with their dagger-like teeth. This was a new slant on nature for me. I was shaken and thrilled all at the same time.

There was that steam whistle again. I asked my father about it and he said it was the quarter-scale train that ran along the west side of the zoo. I was a model train freak. I couldn't believe my ears. This was one of my major fantasies of the time—a real steam model train that you could ride. Wow! This I had to see. I literally dragged the family in that direction. There it was, just behind the merry-go-round (we could get to that later). I stared in disbelief as my father got our tickets. It was a 2-4-0 model from the late 1800s, my favorite period.

While the others found seats on the train, I just stood transfixed next to the engine. It was alive. Heat waves shimmered off the boiler. Live steam hissed from relief valves. A low rumble came from the firebox. The engineer, a slim silver-haired gentleman in his sixties, was checking pressures and adjusting valves. He was dressed in full classic engineer gear—striped coveralls, cap, and red kerchief tied around his neck. Our eyes met. He gave me a knowing smile. No words were necessary.

All this excitement was getting to be too much for a small town boy, but it kept on coming. With lunch at the Cliff House while watching the sea lions, the Palace of Fine Arts, Golden Gate Park and its aroma of eucalyptus trees, cable cars, Fisherman's Wharf—everything had become a blur. I had traveled to the Land of Oz and was very impressed, but just as Dorothy said, "There's no place like home." I don't remember anything about the return trip; I just wanted to be back on my bend in the river.

That summer there was a lot of talk about the V&T railroad—the Virginia and Truckee line connecting Reno and Carson City. The route had been losing money and was going to shut down its operations. My mother told us of taking the V&T all the way to Virginia City in the 1920s with her father. She decided that we children would have a similar story to tell if she took us out to visit my cousins in Washoe Valley on the V&T before it was dismantled. The arrangements were made and the adventure began.

As I remember, the V&T station was near the Southern Pacific tracks in downtown Reno. The tracks went south out of town parallel to Holcomb Avenue, then south along Virginia Street/Highway 395. The two-lane highway crossed and re-crossed the tracks a couple of times before taking off on its own about ten miles south of town. Where the highway starts its long climb up the Washoe Lake hill, the tracks went west to squeeze through a narrow pass, then crossed the highway at right angles at old Washoe City, following the path of the current four-lane highway across Washoe Valley.

The train consisted of two old wooden freight cars and a caboose pulled by a 1920s 0-4-0 steam switch engine. I was in heaven. It was a full-scale model train set. There were no passenger accommodations so we shared the caboose with a portly railroad man who seemed pleased to have the company.

I loved the whole trip. The engine *chug, chug, chugged* in a rapid staccato, pulling us along about thirty miles an hour; its wonderful steam whistle blowing repeatedly at each road crossing. Once we separated from the highway, it was a real Wild West adventure with sweeping vistas of farm and brush country. The train stopped for us at the Flying M. E. Ranch about midway through Washoe Valley. We were met by my Aunt Barbara and spent the rest of the day visiting my cousins. It was a wonderful finish to a great summer.

It was the end of the summer and thoughts of going back to school were in the air. Shopping for new school clothes was a ritual. The dress code was understood by all. Boys were expected to wear leather shoes, a clean button front shirt, and their best Levi's. Girls wore dresses, or skirts with blouses, and school shoes.

Downtown Reno was the only retail and professional district in the area. There were neighborhood grocery stores and gas stations, but all the other consumer item stores were downtown. For school clothes, Sierra Street was the destination. Sears, J.C. Penney, a couple of independent stores, and the upscale department store, Gray Reid and Wright, were all located within two blocks of each other. Parker's Western Wear, on the northeast corner of Center and Second streets, was the best place to buy Levi's.

The stores were all 1920s brick commercial buildings, up to four stories tall and straight out of an Edward Hopper painting. A few examples still exist, but most have been plowed under for casino projects.

The Buster Brown Shoe Store was at the northeast corner of Sierra and Second streets. We usually got shoes at Sears, but we would also have a look at what Buster Brown had to offer. The cool thing at Buster Brown was its x-ray machine. You stood on a platform, placed your feet under a tall box with a greenish screen, and looked down at the screen to see your toes through the new shoes you were trying on. This was before it was known that x-rays were hazardous to your health.

My mother, being a shrewd administrator, always got me shoes at least one size too big, Levi's two inches too long, and shirts one size larger. I arrived at school in these stiff new clothes with rolled up sleeves and cuffs, and shoes that wouldn't start to fit until spring. As soon as I got home from school, it felt great to get into sneakers, a T-shirt, and an old pair of Levi's with patched knees.

I wasn't that excited to be going into second grade. I would still be on the little kids' side of school. I wanted to be with the big kids where the action was.

It was still good to see all the kids I hadn't seen during the summer. There was much information to share and stories to catch up on. Fall has always been a wonderful season in Reno. The warm, calm harvest days with all the beautiful colors is still my favorite time of year. The walk home from school had the bonus of fruit trees in full ripeness. The pears were my favorite. We would arrive home with sticky hands and faces.

School was always good in the fall. First, there was the excitement of seeing all the kids that didn't live in my neighborhood and one or two new kids. Then came Halloween, followed by Thanksgiving, and then Christmas. All three were craft intensive—my best subject. The Halloween ghosts and pumpkins were followed by Thanksgiving pilgrims and turkeys, ending with paper chains and Santas for Christmas, all rendered in colored construction paper and displayed on the classroom windows.

The school Christmas pageant was a big happening. We all had some sort of a part and this year the second graders were supplying the background singing. The district music teacher came once a week and put us through our paces so we would be ready for the big night. She lined us up and had us sing "Jingle Bells." This was great fun. I knew it well and let it all out. The music teacher frowned, had us stop, and then asked us to sing in small groups of four at a time. The first couple of groups did fine, but then it was my group's turn. I once again gave my all. We hadn't done one line when the music teacher exclaimed, "There's the problem!" She had me step out of line and handed me a triangle, telling me that I would not have to sing. Instead I had the special job of ringing the triangle when she gave me the signal.

Christmas was an all-community event. The city put lights on a seventy-foot plus pine tree on Wingfield Park Island. All of downtown was decorated with giant bells, lights, and pine boughs. The whole town surged with American pride.

Selecting our Christmas tree was a family outing—always on December 15th. We usually went to the tree lot run by the Boy Scouts. They had the freshest trees and, my parents thought, the best Christmas spirit. Everyone in the family was given a say-so in the final choice. Then we tied it on the family Ford and headed for home. My father cut the tree so that the Christmas angel's top would just clear the ceiling. The tree was placed in the southwest corner of the living room near the front door.

The decorating of the tree was a full family gig. My parents put the lights on and then everyone hung their favorite ornaments and the paper chains they had made in school. My mother had us string cranberries and make popcorn balls that were also hung on the tree. The icicles in those days were lead foil. They were all stuck together in the package and had to be pulled apart and placed over the branches one strand at a time—this was before they knew that lead was hazardous to your health.

The whole process took hours, but we were so engrossed the time flew by. It was dark when we finished. We turned off all the other lights in the house, stood back, and admired our handiwork. The multicolored lights glistened off the icicles and glass ornaments, enveloping the whole tree in a magical glow. The plaster crèche figures were placed on the mantel, a holly wreath put on the front door, and we were officially Christmas-ready.

Christmas Day was a structured ritual. No matter how hard we tried to be calm and stay in bed, we children were awake and downstairs by six o'clock. It would still be dark outside for another two hours. We each had a stocking hanging off the mantel that we could open and play with, but the presents under the tree had to wait until after breakfast.

Breakfast was at the impossible hour of nine, and if that wasn't frustrating enough, it was also a fancy sit-down breakfast with my grandmother and grandfather Clark. The adults ate slowly, talked, and drank coffee, failing to comprehend the urgency of the situation.

When at last the adults were finished with breakfast, we still had to wait our turn to open a major present. Everyone watched as each present was opened. We children were so hyped on our stocking candy and frustrated by the breakfast delays that we exploded into our presents. Paper went flying and hearts beat quickly.

I got my first pair of figure skates—black lace-up leather boots with silver blades. Wow, I was over the top! The best thing about figure skates was the set of barbs on the front of the blades. You could flip around backwards and stop on a dime in a shower of ice chips—cool.

I got dressed, grabbed my new skates, and headed for my great uncle's pond next door. The pond was a jellybean shape about eighty feet long. It was frozen thick enough to skate on at least three months a year. Yes, the skates were a size too large, but they were so beautiful I didn't really care. I just stuck an extra pair of socks in the toes and went for it. I leapt out on the ice, took two graceful strides, caught the front barbs, and did an ice face-plant.

We skated often that winter. The river was so low that we could rock-hop to Idlewild Park and skate both the large pond and the old swimming pool to the west.

On the weekends there were hundreds of kids and adults skating. People brought logs for warm-up fires so you could skate until your nose and toes were frozen, then thaw out enough by the fire to get back out there. We loved it.

New Year's Eve was the official end to our holiday season. The wreath came off the front door, the Christmas tree was dismantled, and the lights were packed away in the attic. The family was ready to face the new year.

My parents were socially active in the forties and we knew we would be seeing a babysitter on New Year's Eve. They started out at our bedtime. My mother tucked us in, turned out the lights, and casually announced, "See you next year!"

I froze. Will let out a plaintive cry, "*Next year?*" The prospect of being abandoned in the dead of winter was a shock. Betty explained everything and calm was restored.

TWO OR THREE TIMES A WINTER DURING THE forties, enough snow fell that the city closed off Washington and Ralston streets from University to Sixth for sledding. Every kid had a sled. It was usually a hand-me-down from some family member. They were the steel runner, hardwood-slat types one now sees in antique stores. It was great fun. The "steering" bar on the front couldn't really steer the sled, but could make it veer enough to avoid running into others.

We all bundled up with layers of sweaters, coats, mittens, overshoes, and some kind of headgear that covered our ears. We would freeze if we just stood there. After two or three sled runs and pulling our sleds back up the hill, we were toasty.

The little kids sat on the sled between the legs of an adult, started slowly from the top of the hill, and wound their way down. If you were eight, you most likely had an old candle stub in your pocket to wax the runners.

Then you picked up your sled, got well back from the top of the hill, ran for all you were worth, threw your sled out in front of you, and leapt onto it in mid-air. Flying down the hill in a prone position with your nose six inches off the snow was a rush.

My eighth birthday put me one year away from the bicycle of my choice. My mother had an ironclad rule concerning bicycles. We were not to have our own bicycle before the age of nine. This was frustrating because all of us could ride a bicycle by the time we were six. But the bright spot of this birthday was my growth spurt. In the last year, I had grown three inches and change and now had four silver dollars from my grandfather to prove it. The extra inches made my legs just long enough to reach the peddles of a car if I had a pillow behind my back.

At the time, Chism's Auto Camp had a 1932 Ford pick-up truck. I loved that truck. It was all "form follows function." It had black fenders, a tan body, V8 engine, and side-mounted spare tire. Whenever it wasn't in use, I could be found sitting in the driver's seat shifting the gears, pushing the pedals, and producing the appropriate noises. It was my driving simulator. In years past I was allowed to steer while sitting in my father's lap, but now that I could reach the pedals, I was determined to drive on my own.

My mother loved all the traditional holidays of the year, but I think her favorite was Easter. Decorating Easter eggs combined all her craft talents and was something all of us kids could do as well. She would boil dozens of eggs, clear the dining table, and put Easter egg dye in every bowl we owned. We would spend days creating just before Easter. There were many colors of dye to choose from, along with paint brushes, watercolors, India ink, and crayons. Glue and colored paper were available to put ears, collars, and hair on our egg art. We loved it because there was no right or wrong way to do an Easter egg and originality was applauded.

My mother organized an Easter egg hunt for the children of the auto camp, as well as a private hunt for our family. The auto camp hunt was held in the park next to the office. The parents hid the eggs very early in the morning and then, when all the kids arrived, the one- to three-year-olds were the first to hunt, with lots

Easter egg hunting at the Chism's Auto Camp – 1948

of encouragement from the sidelines. After about twenty minutes, the older kids were let loose. Prizes were given for finding the gold and silver eggs—a great time was had by all.

Our family hunt was usually held in the front yard of our house, but one Easter it was so cold and rainy that my mother had the Easter egg hunt in our front room. My parents found some clever places to hide eggs and we delighted in finding eggs where no one would think an egg could be hidden. The indoor hunt was a great success. About a month later, though, the front room took on a bit of a pong. There was this smell that no one could identify. A couple of eggs had been so cunningly hidden that only a smelly rot revealed their whereabouts.

Reno was on the move. The first housing subdivision in town was being constructed. There was much adult conversation on the subject—houses being built in large batches of the same design? What was becoming of the individual? What would become of our town if this was allowed to continue?

The offending development was Westfield Village and was only about three quarters of a mile from our house as the goose flies. My parents had new friends, the Vhays, who lived right next to the project. David Vhay was an architect and he and his wife, Mel, had two children, David and Diana. David, known as Tink by everyone, was very close to my age. Even better, Tink was into model trains, guns, building things, and great adventures of the imagination. Wow! We hit it off from our first meeting.

The Vhays had purchased a turn-of-the-century farmhouse with a long fieldstone milking barn just south of their house and bordering Westfield Village. Their plan was to rebuild the milking barn into their family home, but for the time being their family of four was living in the small two-bedroom farmhouse. Tink's father turned the hall closet into Tink's bedroom. His bed filled the whole closet, but was suspended five feet up and had a ladder. This created a hideout effect. There was a little slit window providing ventilation and a bunker-like observation post of the area around the

Me and Tink Vhay

house. The space under the bed was storage for all of Tink's stuff. It was heaven to an eight-year-old.

Since our parents got together now and then for drinks and card playing, Tink and I had time to collect construction scraps from the houses being built next door in Westfield Village. We had our fort projects to build. We also explored the large open field that spread north of their house to the power company flume that bordered Idlewild Park. This large field was to become the site of the new Reno High School. Excavations had already begun.

The big event for my family in 1948 was that we got a new car. My mother's grandfather had passed away and left her two thousand dollars, a princely sum for the time. The car was a Chevrolet station wagon. The stately height of the main body, with its lustrous hardwood construction, was preceded by a metallic green streamlined hood and sensuous pontoon-like front fenders. A rocket ship hood ornament and a forceful chrome grill topped off the whole package. Part stagecoach, part car, it was perfect for the high desert West.

The new car spawned an explosion of family trips. We really didn't all fit into the old Ford business coupe. We now had the open road laid out before us. A favorite trip was a visit to my uncle Walter and my cousins, Babs and Bobby.

Uncle Walter leased a wonderful nineteenth-century ranch house in Washoe Valley. It was a good-sized frame house of two stories just at the timberline on the west

Clark, Chism, and Santini Family Photo – 1946

TOP ROW: *James Santini, Walter Clark Sr., Euphemia Santini, Walter Clark, Marge Clark, Miriam Chism (hidden), David Clark.* MIDDLE ROW: *Betty Chism, David Chism (in arms of Barbara Clark), Euphemia Clark.* BOTTOM ROW: *Will Chism, Clark Santini, Bobby Clark, Gordon Chism, Babs Clark, J.D. Santini.* SEATED: *John Chism.*

side of the valley. It was like something out of *National Geographic*. In those days, Washoe Valley was essentially cattle grasslands on the west side of Washoe Lake and open brush land on the east. There were no more than a hundred people living in the valley year-round. Babs and Bobby attended the last one-room schoolhouse in the state—first through sixth grades. It was just off the Franktown Road and looked out over the valley. The little school was of white frame construction with a bell tower. Motion picture set designers couldn't have done a better job.

My cousins' house faced east with a panoramic view over the valley. Directly behind the house was a large horse barn where my uncle had his writing studio. To the north of the barn was a blacksmith's shop with all the original tools, bellows, anvils, and hammers. It was a time capsule. The thing that impressed me most was a penny-farthing bicycle hanging from the ceiling.

Babs and Bobby were super cousins. At ten, Babs was not only an accomplished horse rider, but also rode with the Heidenreich cattle ranchers on round-ups. My sister Betty loved horses and was green with envy.

On one of our visits, I asked my aunt Barbara if Bobby could come out and play. She said yes, but not until he had finished transcribing his father's notes. In the background, I could hear a typewriter tapping away at an impressive rate. Since we were the same age and I was just getting a handle on *Dick, Jane, and Spot*, I was more than impressed. Even though my cousins were participating in the adult world, they were still very much kids. We played cowboys and Indians, Civil War, and explorer. They were a good time.

My mother had dropped the dollhouse craft project and was now taking painting courses at the University of Nevada. She also decided to redecorate the front room and dining room of our house. The hokey wagon wheel couch set was to go to the Clark family cabin at Lake Tahoe and would be replaced by a new upholstered easy chair and couch of a sage green material. She had the front room carpeted wall-to-wall and laid green marbled asphalt tile over the hardwood floor in the dining room. We were going totally modern.

During this period, my mother frequently visited second-hand shops—the 1940s version of the garage sale. There were a dozen second hand/used furniture shops scattered along a half-mile strip of Prater Way in Sparks, starting where Prater Way branches off Fourth Street. These were usually Mom-and-Pop operations, where more often than not the proprietors lived on the premises. The shops were unheated barn-like structures that sold everything—bins and bins of everything.

My mother knew half of the proprietors on a first-name basis. When she went a-hunting she took us kids along. The shops were full of old energy—spent but begging to be recycled. As part of the front room redecoration, she purchased a round claw-foot oak dining table for eight dollars. I remember the price because my mother haggled over it for two or three visits.

With the aid of my father, the old oak table's pedestal was cut about in half and became the coffee table that

my parents used in their conversation area for the rest
of their lives. My parents were products of the Great
Depression, which meant saving money and creating
something out of nothing was an established way of life.

We kept hearing about television. Sets could be seen
in the windows of appliance stores downtown. When we
did get a look at an operating TV, it had fuzzy reception
and the only thing on was a test pattern. Even the test
pattern was on only a few hours a day. The adult view
was that trash programming would ruin young minds.
My mother declared that there would never be a TV in
our house.

During the summer of '48, the adult world was abuzz
with political speculation. President Truman was to run
against the Republican nominee in the 1948 election.
My parents were so stirred up that they felt they had to
watch the first televised political conventions. Since
Reno had no national hook-up at the time, they decided
to go to Sacramento and get a hotel room with a TV.
They hired a babysitter for us and went off in an excited
rush. If television was this important to my parents, I
knew it had to be something very special.

At this time, my uncle David was building a house
out in the country farther west of our house. Today it
would be the heights halfway between Highway 80 and
Fourth Street and just east of the McCarran Boulevard
ring route. In the forties this area had two or three little
farms, but was mostly sagebrush country.

Uncle David was doing a sort of back-to-basics
venture. He put in a good-sized lawn and a large vege-

table garden on his two acres. He spent the better part of the next three years trying to keep the jackrabbits and the range cattle out of his garden.

These days it is hard to think of a place within the McCarran rim route of Reno as being out in the country, but in the forties my uncle's house was definitely out in the country. The only way to get to his property was up a very steep dirt road that traversed the face of the heights. It was so steep that often in the winter no one could get up or down. Once on top, the one-track dirt road went in a series of right angle turns around Mrs. Smith's goat farm, then over the cattle guard, and onto my uncle's property. In those days there was no access to the land northwest of Reno. It was just untracked brush country.

The house itself was essentially a studio apartment above a two-car garage and shop. A large east-facing deck ran the length of the building and featured a great view of the city. Uncle David and Aunt Marge had no children of their own, but often had our family over and seemed to enjoy having us kids around. One day while we were visiting, my uncle asked if I would like to go flying with him in the morning.

Wow! Would I like to go flying with him? My dream of dreams was to be a pilot. The sooner I got started the better. Uncle David picked me up just before seven o'clock a.m.—we were on the dawn patrol. My uncle had earned his pilot's license the year before at the Joe Williams Flight School at the Reno Municipal Airport. He rented one of the three Aeronca Seven airplanes in the Joe Williams Flight School fleet. The Aeronca Seven was very similar to the Piper Cub that was so popular just after the war.

As we pushed the little yellow plane out of the hangar and into the morning light, my heart began to race. There was an intoxicating smell—part aviation fuel, part fabric dope. We went on a short walk around the plane to make sure all of the control surfaces were in working order. We got into the plane. It was a cramped, tandem two-seater. I got in the back and my uncle made sure that I was strapped in tight. He then buckled into the front seat and Joe Williams himself grabbed the prop. "Brakes on," shouted Joe Williams. "Brakes on," replied my uncle. "Switch off," said Joe. "Switch off," repeated my uncle. I felt like I was in an adventure movie. Joe turned the prop over twice, then— "Contact." "Contact," declared my uncle. A twist of the propeller and the engine came to life. I was in a state of rapture.

I sat just tall enough to see over the edge of the Plexiglas side windows. I was all aglow as we taxied to the end of the runway. My uncle put the brakes on and ran the little engine to top revs on one magneto, than the other. This was all part of the preflight ritual. The plane had a radio, but it could only receive. The reception was so static-ridden due to the engine's magneto, it was virtually useless. We had to look to the windows of the control tower for permission to take off. The tower gave us the green light—literally. The traffic controller had a powerful directional light that he aimed at us.

My uncle lined us up on the north/south runway and gave the engine full throttle. A great roar built steadily as the little plane gathered speed, the tail came up, and we were flying! I was only eight and I was flying!

We labored to a thousand feet and headed south toward Washoe Valley. I was enthralled. I could see the tiny cows of the dairies that were near the airport and the tiny cars of people going to work on the roads below. It was truly a bird's eye view. I knew the land below well, but it was very different from above. We passed over Little Washoe Lake then off to the west of the valley.

My uncle yelled something to me over his shoulder, but the steady roar of the engine made conversation impossible. He then put the plane into a steep turn, dipping the wing toward the ground, causing the plane to pull at least three Gs. Blood pulled from my head and seemed to pool in my stomach. I suddenly realized that there below was my uncle Walter's house.

We made one complete circle. A heavy blanket of centrifugal force pushed me down into my seat and made my head and arms heavy. While we were in the middle of the second circle, a tiny person came out of the house, then another, until Uncle Walter, Aunt Barbara, Babs, and Bobby were looking up and waving at us. I waved back even though I felt that after one more circle I might lose my breakfast.

I had a broader focus during the flight back as I became acclimated to the constant vibration and roar of the engine. The valley and the Sierras were quite beautiful from this new perspective. We approached the Reno Airport on the east side of the north/south runway, known as the downwind leg of the landing pattern.

When we got about even with the tower, we received another green light and my uncle waved the wings in acknowledgment. We made two left ninety-degree turns and came in to land.

During the whole time we were taxiing out, taking off, landing, and taxiing back to the hangar, we were the only active aircraft. Being an air traffic controller at the Reno Municipal Airport was not a stressful occupation in 1948.

Usually my uncle practiced his turns and spin recoveries when he took me flying. There was a maneuver called a *chandelle*, which consisted of pulling the plane into such a steep climb that the wings would stall out; then my uncle would kick the rudder, putting the plane into a diving spin. The experience is hard to explain. The steep climb pulls the blood from your head, then the stall causes the plane to fall, leaving your stomach suspended. The spin is an asymmetric centrifuge sort of thing that causes your head and stomach fluids to spin to the outside. At this point we were out of control—spinning straight into the ground. With rudder and stick guiding a blood-draining pullout, my uncle got the little plane leveled off. Then we climbed up and did it again.

Sometimes we went out in the afternoon. The winds were so strong that the little plane would all but stand still when we tried to go west. The turbulence would throw us a hundred feet up or down without warning. I was still determined to be a hero aviator and I took pride in the fact that I never did throw up in the plane. I was reluctant to admit that, after many flying dates with my uncle, the reality of flying was quite different from my fantasies of flying. I wanted to wave to earthbound inferiors as I sped past, skimming the treetops. I wanted to wear all the cool leather aviation gear and save beautiful girls, but I discovered that aviation was not the romantic experience I had envisioned. It was heavily regulated, exacting, and head-poundingly noisy.

In the 1940s, groceries were sold by dozens of little Mom & Pop stores that were within walking distance of the various residential neighborhoods. There were larger grocery stores in the downtown area, but nothing resembling the supermarkets of today. Most everyone dealt with their neighborhood store and in our case it was Bricky's, about four blocks east of our house.

Bricky's was a '30s grocery store of about fifteen hundred square feet located on West Second Street between Winter and Washington streets. It had a curved stucco facade and a sagging wooden screen door sporting a Coca-Cola push bar. As you entered, the slap of the screen door hit just as you drew even with the gray marble-topped sales counter on your left. Behind the counter to the back of the store was Charley the butcher and his little shop within the store. The back wall was green groceries, and the remaining bulk of the store was handmade wooden shelves painted hospital green holding bright boxes, bottles, and cans.

Bricky was a heavy-set man in his late thirties. He always wore a smudged white apron and a big smile with a cigar stuck in one corner of his mouth. His face was an off-white pink, dominated by a long sharp nose, and topped by a head of thinning red hair. Bricky loved people and laughter. He would play with us kids and joke with the adults. Everybody knew Bricky and Bricky knew every man, woman, and child in the area. It was a personal and enjoyable way to procure our necessities of life. Charley the butcher gave us pork fat scraps for crawdad fishing and we would often buy penny candy for our summertime adventures.

We kids also saved our pennies for the army and navy surplus store just north of the tracks on Arlington Street. It was a turn-of-the-century brick store of about a thousand square feet with fifteen-foot ceilings. It was our wonderland. War surplus everything was sold for far less than a penny on the dollar. Wonderful useless military goods of almost infinite variety were hung from the ceiling, stacked in piles, and stuffed in bins. There were hundreds of inflatable life preservers with the pilots' names still on them for ten cents each. Helmet liners topped every war-playing kid's head. These looked just like the American helmet, but were the fiber liner that suspended the steel helmet above one's head.

Another must was trenching tools. They came in two types—my favorites were the miniature pick and shovel. They were kid-sized but serious tools. Every kid had an army web belt with cartridge pockets and a canteen. There were K-rations, caps, hats, helmets, flashlights, unit patches, socks, shirts, pants, boots, gas masks, and on and on. A kid could barely carry out all he could buy with a dollar.

Being typical children, we pressured our parents for a dog. Promises were made but never fulfilled. Then in the spring of '48, my mother announced that we were going on a family outing to look at collie pups on a ranch in Washoe Valley. There were nine pups that were only about three weeks old. They were all irresistible. Multicolored powder puffs with little black noses romped around, wagging their tails. My mother insisted that we pick a female. We finally agreed on a shy lovable pup we named Karen, for reasons I can't remember. On the way home Karen got carsick and threw up.

We were now the complete American family. We had the family home, the station wagon, four children, and a dog. Life was good. Life was good for everyone we knew. Friends of my parents would drive by when they got a new car. The man would lift the hood and explain the technical wonders to my father while us kids fought for a window seat for the upcoming drive through town. There was a solid sense of American pride and optimism in the Reno area.

Family outings were far easier with our new station wagon. It had three rows of seats and a little cargo area behind the last row. The interior resembled a wooden cabin cruiser. The ceiling was exposed wooden cross-ribs with thin wood strips that supported the fabric roof. The doors and the cabin were thick hardwood frames with plywood panels. It was the last year that real wooden station wagons were built. Now we all could fit in the family car including the newest member, Karen.

The Clark and Chism families trekked out to Pyramid Lake at least twice a summer. Grandmother Clark, Uncle Walter, Aunt Barbara, and my cousins Babs and Bobby; Uncle David and Aunt Marge, and our family made a lively group. They were the best of times. We caravaned out in three cars and set up a base camp at the tufa formations on the west side of the lake above the marine bushes. The drought had a large impact on Pyramid Lake. It was much lower than when my mother was a child in the 1920s. She told us about diving off the tufa rocks into the lake. We just couldn't believe her.

When we were at the lake and other people showed up, the adults would mumble, "How rude." We were accustomed to having the lake all to ourselves, and anyone else was an interloper. If a party set up camp within sight of another party that was already there, they were considered to be in poor taste.

We swam all afternoon. We kids found black clay deposits just under the water and used it for war paint. Uncle David would throw us up in the air in the deeper water and dunk us until we laughed and screamed for mercy. My father and Uncle Walter would swim out a quarter of a mile, which impressed me. Since I was so skinny, I sank in the water like a stone. When we were all exhausted and the shadows were getting long, we'd gather around the campfire for the evening meal.

As the sun began to set, the surreal beauty of the lake would cause everyone to reflect in silence. If my family had a spiritual place it was surely Pyramid Lake. This great body of water (larger than Lake Tahoe) in the stark high desert, bordered by treeless rugged mountains, couldn't help but move the soul. With the setting of the sun, the adults would sing. Uncle Walter had a bass voice and my mother had a strong clear complementary voice. It was enough to bring a tear to the eye.

Another summer favorite was a trip to Bower's Mansion. In the forties, the west half of Washoe Valley was cattle country. There was no commercial presence, just beautiful green pastures sloping up into the pine-covered Sierra mountains. It was only a half-hour drive from Reno, and Uncle Walter and his family lived just five minutes away.

The mansion was much the same as it is now, but the grounds and swimming pool were quite different. In the forties, the entire place had the look and feel of a do-it-yourself-project. To the northeast of the mansion, there was a small dance pavilion with a covered bandstand. My parents talked of dances once held there during their high school and college years. To the south side of the mansion, a picnic area of wooden tables and native stone cooking grills became our base camp.

To the north was the swimming pool, which was really three pools. The first pool was filled with water straight out of the hot spring. It was about twenty feet in diameter and wicked hot. I couldn't stay in it. The second pool was just downhill from the first, but much larger, around fifty feet across with an island in the middle. It was still on the hot side, but bearable. That's where little kids and old folks waded about. The big pool was about twice as large as the second and was comfortably warm and deep enough for diving. The sides of the pools were concrete, but the bottoms were sand. These old pools still exist behind a tall wooden fence.

There were other pools in the area—Idlewild Park Municipal Pool, Moana Hot Springs, and the YMCA, but because the polio scare was still prevalent, my parents didn't want us swimming in crowded public pools.

Bower's Mansion was always fun. The hot dogs, hamburgers, watermelon, and my cousins created a *good* time, but add the swimming and hiking in the mountains just behind the mansion and you had a *great* time. There was a sense of family history and a feeling of belonging.

By the end of the summer of '48, I was working with my father and the hired man maintaining Chism's Auto Camp. The fences were always in need of repair and keeping seven acres raked and picked up was a never-ending job. I got my first taste of driving the old Ford pick-up around the auto camp. At first I was only trusted to go forty feet between rake-up piles, but by the time school started I was driving solo all over the camp.

Maintenance at Chism's Auto Camp usually necessitated a trip to the hardware store. For our hardware needs, we had a charge account at Reno Mercantile. It was a wonderful hardware store—a sort of 1900s time capsule—at the corner of Commercial Row and Sierra Street. The storefront on Commercial Row had a glass and wood door that was nine feet high with glass display areas on either side. The Sierra Street side of the building was windowless. The building itself was a great example of a brick commercial building from the turn of the century. We always entered through the back door off Sierra Street.

Upon entering, there was a period of adjustment. Going from the bright outdoors into the cavernous gloom of the interior stopped you in your tracks. The main floor was about sixty by twenty feet with twenty-foot ceilings. I was fascinated by the hardwood ladders that ran on tracks, gliding back and forth along the floor-to-ceiling shelves. These ladders allowed access to the hardware goods that were fifteen feet up the wall. The rest of the room contained freestanding display cases aligned in military rows.

If you were looking for a hardware item, it was surely there somewhere. Once in a while we needed an industrial-sized bolt or a keg of nails and the salesperson would lead us into the pitch black basement. From the light of a bare bulb we could see the massive wooden beams that supported the main floor. Skulking about in the gloom were crates with massive bolts of various sizes, water and sewer pipe, coils of steel cable, and large diameter rope. The walls were stone and the floor was dirt. It was right out of a horror movie.

The sales counter was a wide hardwood surface with a large roll of thin glossy brown paper to the left. When a sale was made, a length of brown paper was pulled from the roll; purchases were placed in the middle of the paper and wrapped into a bundle, then tied with string. An experienced salesperson could wrap and tie in three or four seconds. There were no plastic bags in those days.

My father had an affinity for breakfast rolls, so on Sunday mornings I went with him to get lemon snails and bear claws. The bakery was two doors east of Reno Mercantile on Commercial Row and could have been another 1900s movie set. It was about twenty feet wide with the entrance in the middle, flanked by storefront windows on each side. The windows had white curtains over their lower half. The bakery interior had scrubbed white tile halfway up the walls and mosaic black and white tile floor. About six feet inside the door, glass display cases ran straight across the shop.

Just a quick scan of those display cases made a boy's mouth water. Cakes, pies, cookies, donuts, rolls, breads—the warmth and delicious smell of baking filled the room. You couldn't help but get a feeling of well being. The servers were pleasant Nordic women with rosy cheeks and big smiles. With a little coaxing, I could get my father to buy me a single cookie of my choosing to tide me over until we got back home.

I started the third grade that fall. It would be my last year on the little kids' side of school. The game of marbles was becoming more and more important, and was the measure of a boy in grammar school. You had to be a competitive player by the time you were in fourth grade or you just didn't count.

After about two months, I was playing marbles, but I was of the flipper rather than the shooter school. I was holding the marble in the crook of my index finger and flipping the marble out with my thumbnail—bad form.

All the hotshots balanced the marble on the tip of their index finger and their thumb knuckle, then used their middle finger to release the thumb under pressure— Pow!

I confided my playground embarrassment to my father. It turned out that he was as good at marbles as he was at ice-skating. Within a week of practicing on the living room carpet, he had me shooting with the best of them. By the end of the year I was the terror of the third grade.

Uncle Walter was an avid fan of University of Nevada basketball. He brought his family in from Washoe Valley to watch the games. My parents made it a family get-together by taking us all to the games as well. To us kids this was as big-time as sports got. We always sat just to the side of one of the backboards in the second-floor seating. The games were well attended, so we had to get there early enough to get the good seats. This gave us time to run around exploring the stadium with our cousins before the game started.

The games were colorful, loud, and exciting. Will and I dreamed that we would someday be basketball players for our schools and drove our mother crazy bouncing our basketball in the house. We needed to take it outside. At our urgent request, our father erected a basketball hoop and backboard at the north end of our backyard. For the next ten years, the Chism boys played thousands of hours of horse, dreaming of peer-group glory.

With no TV yet, the movies were a big deal. During our childhood, there were four theaters in downtown

Reno—the Tower, the Majestic, the Granada, and the just-opened Crest.

Saturdays were kiddie matinees at the Tower Theater. The price of admission was three bottle caps from Crescent Creamery milk bottles. (Yes, the milk was home delivered and came in glass bottles—our family got seven quarts each morning.) The Tower Theater was on the east side of Virginia Street between Pine and Ryland and next door to a bowling alley. All during the movie, you could hear the *plink* of the ball hitting the pins and the *crash* of the pins being reset.

There were cartoons, an adventure movie from the thirties, and a serial. The serial was usually a *Captain America, Flash Gordon, Sky King* or some crime-fighting cop show. The theater was always abuzz with childish excitement, but I don't remember any fights or riots. Kids in the forties had self control even when they were not directly supervised.

We would also go by ourselves to first-run movies on Saturday afternoons. Betty was in charge. The Majestic and the Granada were both on First Street. The Majestic was on the southwest corner of First and Center streets and was the grand dame of local movie theaters. It was not only the largest, but also had a balcony and a stage in front of the screen. It had been a silent theater in the twenties, with grandiose medieval murals on the walls and a huge chandelier hanging over the main floor seats. I can remember as a child looking up at that chandelier and thinking of the carnage it would cause if it should fall.

The Granada was on the south side of First Street between Sierra and Virginia streets. The Granada was a more contemporary theater than the Majestic, with a more restrained interior. Most of the first-run movies played at the Majestic or the Granada, while the Tower played mostly B movies. The new theater in town—the Crest—put itself forward as the "better," more modern theater. It was toward the west end on the north side of Second Street between Sierra and Virginia streets. The Crest had less than half the seating capacity of the Majestic or the Granada so it charged more for a ticket. This greatly upset us junior moviegoers.

My parents picked us up after we called them on the lobby payphone when the movie was over. Our home phone number was 2-4-3-5-3 and after a really exciting movie it was hard to remember. I am sure our parents treasured our times at the movies.

The fall and winter of '48 were extremely cold and ice-skating was in full swing by late November. During recess and lunchtime we made huge snowmen on the front lawn of the school and carried on snowball fights as we did.

All the kids had galoshes over their shoes. When recess was over, there would be five to ten minutes of removing our snow gear in the cloakroom. Behind the teacher's desk, each home room had a cloakroom of about four by twenty feet with a door at each end. There were about twenty-five coat hooks at child level and each child was assigned one. On snowy days, the floor

would be awash in melt. Spirits were running high with
the expectations of Christmas, Christmas vacation, and
the coming new year.

MY FATHER WAS A MEMBER OF THE OPTIMISTS Club. In the forties, most of the men of my family's acquaintance were members of a service club. There were Lions, Rotary, Optimists, and four or five others I can't remember. The Optimists met for lunch weekly at the Hotel El Cortez. They held a father/son luncheon once a year and 1949 was the year I was to go.

The Hotel El Cortez was a late twenties, early thirties small hotel on the northeast corner of West Second and Arlington streets. The meeting room was good-sized and decorated in the Art Deco mode, with indirect lighting inside the exaggerated cove molding around the edges, and flying-saucer-like light fixtures hanging in the middle of the room.

I was feeling strange all dressed up in my suit. I looked around the room and could see that the other boys were just as uncomfortable as I was. The lunch was breaded veal cutlets, mashed potatoes, and peas. It had a generous dollop of white gravy and was nothing like a meal we would have at home. I thought it was great.

One by one the members rose and introduced their sons. There was a feeling of inclusion, that one day I would be an Optimist introducing my son—continuing the tradition. After the lunch, there was much parliamentary procedure. They were making plans for the Reno Fourth of July Rodeo, the richest rodeo in the West. The Optimists ran the concession stands to fund their main charity, a summer camp for underprivileged boys. All of this took place in a cloud of cigarette smoke. There was an ashtray in front of every place setting.

Today it is hard to understand how pervasive smoking was. My father and mother smoked, as did most every adult I knew. Our family doctor smoked and his waiting room had a number of standing ashtrays. Every public place had cigarettes for sale or a cigarette machine. Everyone's house smelled of cigarettes. The smell of tobacco smoke, along with a hint of bacon grease, was so typical that it symbolized a home—a sort of greeting when a front door was opened. At the movies, the smoke was so thick that you could see the projector beam from the back of the theater to the screen. In school, we made clay ashtrays for our parents' Christmas presents. Smoking accessories, ashtrays, lighters, and cigarette boxes were always a safe gift for anyone over eighteen.

It was almost spring and I had finally reached my ninth birthday. It was time for the bicycle of my choice. I got another four dollars for growth from my grandfather Clark and my apple pie with nine candles. I was not a cake person.

In the forties, bicycles were a child-only item. Few adults rode bicycles. The choice was all fat tires, chrome, and streamlined front fender lights. The bicycle shop (the Schwinn dealer) was on Fourth Street and Lake. My father took me down to the Schwinn shop and waited for me to pick one out. I had a hard time with all the chrome accessories as they made the bike heavier and I valued performance. I finally picked out a little red bike with smaller diameter wheels and a small peddle sprocket. I could out-accelerate every kid on the block. I took the fenders off to make it lighter and turned the handlebars upside down to make it easier to ride no-hands. I now had personal transportation and my world was expanding.

My new bicycle made it easier to share my friendship with Tink Vhay. The Vhay family had just moved into their renovated stone milking barn. It made a much more comfortable house than their little red farmhouse. Now Tink had his own bedroom and room for his train set. We had much to discuss, plan, and implement.

We were both changing from O gauge model trains to HO. The HO trains were half the size of the Lionel train sets that most kids had in the forties. The HO trains were light-years ahead of the O gauge sets in accuracy, detail, and commitment. We didn't just buy railroad cars in HO, but instead built them from model kits. The tracks weren't just plugged together; we had to fasten them to a layout board. There were also scale building kits, cast metal men, and cars—you were creating a whole world in miniature. Tink and I would get together, build HO pieces, and discuss the latest goings-on in *Popular Mechanics*. We also went exploring on foot and bicycle. Fort-building and shooting bows and arrows were other shared interests.

Next to Tink's house, work was starting in earnest on the new Reno High School. With a lot of heavy equipment to watch and admire, the whole project was of the new America scale—too big to believe. The old Reno High School, built in the early 1900s, was on two-thirds of a city block between Arlington and West streets off Fifth Street. The new Reno High School was on seventy-plus acres. It was to be the biggest building in Reno, with extensive playing fields, football stadium, and a separate Industrial Arts complex.

My mother's new interest in painting classes was changing our family's social dynamics. The professors of the university art department started coming to our house for drinks after class. They were wonderful people—Craig Sheppard, Ed Yates, and their wives and children. Tink's parents were also part of the new social order. The Sheppard's children, Sophie and Shep, were a couple of years younger than Tink and me, but they were good fun anyway. Our family trips to Pyramid Lake now became art group picnics.

Craig Sheppard was the sparkplug of the new alliance and a mentor to Tink and me. He was handsome, energetic, humorous, and creative. Craig was into guns, art, building kites, and having a good time. The Sheppards lived in the new Westfield Village development, about two blocks from Tink's house.

The new bathhouse and laundry at Chism's Auto Camp was completed and the old bathhouse and laundry was now the new maintenance shop area. The old clothes-drying yard to the south of the old laundry was taken down and a new one erected to the north of the new bathhouse, taking up about a third of the park area. All this reconfiguration was an in-house project with a labor force of the hired man, my father, and me. I was also the summertime maintenance man for the men's bathhouse—not my favorite duty at the auto camp.

The Fourth of July parade was the biggest of the year. In the forties, parades were a community gathering. The people in the crowd knew many of the people in the parade and were related to a few. Parades were a chance for all of the community clubs, organizations, and dignitaries to strut their stuff. There were service clubs, Boy and Girl Scouts, horse-riding clubs, high school and college ROTC, the Nevada National Guard, high school bands, fire departments, and on and on. It was a regional celebration as well, as smaller outlying towns attended with their high school bands and civic organizations.

The stars of the parade were the cowboys, the sheriff's mounted posse, and the rodeo queen and her court. Since western movies were so big, the grand marshal of the parade was usually a western movie star. Excitement was in the air and everyone was proud to be an American.

At our house, a small flagpole holder was just to the left of our front door. We would fly our American flag on the Fourth of July, Armistice Day, Washington's birthday, etc. It was a common practice of the time.

From year to year the parade route changed, but the reviewing stand was invariably on Virginia Street in front of the library. My father told the story of how in the late twenties he carried the American flag at the head of the Fourth of July parade. He was in the Reno High School ROTC and led the entire parade. The parade formed on West Commercial Row, then turned right onto Virginia Street heading south.

There was a stiff breeze blowing north up Virginia Street that day. As the band played, my father turned the corner carrying Old Glory. The flag was a large one. The breeze caught it like a sail, over-powering his one-hundred-and-forty-pound frame. The parade stopped as my father was blown backwards over the railroad tracks in the wrong direction. The crowd gasped. My father regained his footing, lowered the flag into the wind, and battled his way back across the tracks. The crowd let out a cheer and the parade was on again.

The Fourth of July parade marked the kick-off for the Reno Rodeo, known as Cowboy Christmas, which was the highest paying rodeo of the time. The rodeo took place on the north side of town, the present site of the Washoe County Fairgrounds off north Wells Avenue. In the forties, the fairgrounds consisted of a large horseracing track, horse barns, and grandstands. The horserace track had been active in the twenties, but the only structures still maintained in the forties were the grandstands and the rodeo arena.

My father selling beer and pop at the Reno Rodeo

Weather on the Fourth of July was invariably hot and dry. The rodeo arena was dusty and heavy with a barnyard scent. The people in the crowds were primarily country folks from all over the state. They had come to cheer on their local heroes and celebrate the western way of life. The excitement was physical and social—a heady brew.

As I had proven myself to be useful at Chism's Auto Camp, I was invited along to help my father and the Optimists Club sell pop and beer to the crowds. The rodeo was a weeklong affair so there was a lot to do. My father sold the pop and beer to the people in the stands and I was the bucket man. I went down under the grandstands to the storage area to get a bucket of beer and a bucket of pop, cover them with ice, and take them back up to my father in the stands. Then I took the empty buckets back down, keeping up this routine all day. It was hard work, but I was one of the guys, a hard-working Optimist.

At the time, there was a state law prohibiting the sale of alcohol to full-blooded Indians. The Optimists took a liberal interpretation of this law so were very popular with the many Indians that came to the rodeo. The men addressed the Indians as "my Mexican friend" when selling them beer. The old infield of the racetrack was dotted with Indian campsites. The Indians bought whole cases of beer at the retail price, making a windfall profit for the Optimists.

At home, Karen, our collie pup of a year ago, had grown to full size. She regarded my siblings and me as her puppies—her responsibility. She followed us around to make sure we didn't get into trouble. She loved to play and could easily out-wrestle us if she wanted to, but preferred to nanny us instead.

The summer was hot and polio was still a concern. Swimming in public pools was thought to be a poor idea. Although we couldn't afford it, my mother took us once a week to Laughton Hot Springs to cool off. Laughton's was an up-scale swimming pool complex about four miles west of town on the Truckee River.

It was fun because it was like a Hollywood set done in California Mission style. The pool was Olympic-size with a connecting tile roof, white stucco dressing rooms, concession stand, and private hot tubs to the east, south, and west, forming a Spanish-style fort. The west end of the pool had the deepest water and the diving boards.

We all used the low diving board, but the high board was a real think piece—ten feet to the water. There was also a stucco diving tower about twelve-feet square with a pointed tile roof. It had diving platforms at ten, twenty, and thirty feet. Luckily, the diving tower was closed to everyday use. It took me months to do the high board and the diving tower was beyond my courage level.

The north of the pool was open to a grass park with shade trees. Up an embankment, the Southern Pacific tracks and Highway 80 passed by the park.

My uncle Walter's best friend during his youth was an artist named Robert Caples. He was straight out of a Fitzgerald novel—tall, elegant, philosophical, quiet, handsome, and intelligent. We all regarded him with a sense of awe. He was the shaman of our tribe. His paintings of the Nevada mountains were nothing short of spiritual. He eloquently captured the grandeur and mystery of the high desert. He dropped by our house a couple of times a year to have a drink and talk to my parents and then at other times we made a family outing to visit him. I loved these trips because Robert Caples always had a great alternative housing situation going on. Being an artist in the forties meant an acceptance of poverty, but he made it seem fun and exciting.

In 1949, Robert Caples lived in an outlying cabin at Carson Hot Springs. In those days, Carson Hot Springs was a mile north of Carson City in a sea of sagebrush. The cabin was a white one-room clapboard affair, about sixteen by twenty feet. His cot was in one corner and a small table with two chairs stood against the far wall. The rest of the room was his painting studio. There were dozens of soup cans on the floor, each containing a different paint color. There were many stretched canvases and works in progress leaning against the wall, and his current project was up on his easel.

I idolized Robert Caples. He was a respected adult, but he lived his own version of life and made it work. Post-war America was very much a "do-what-is-expected-of-you-and-don't-rock-the-boat" kind of world. Robert Caples showed me that a person could go his own way and still be a valued member of the community.

In the summer of '49, I got my first rifle. This was big. There was still a code of the West—a man was required to know his firearms. My father was an exception to this rule. He just didn't like guns. He told me of going duck hunting with one of his uncles when he was in his teens. As they were getting out of the car, one of the men in the hunting party turned to my father and said, "Son, you are out huntin'—shoot anything big enough to die."

Craig Sheppard gave me a Savage .22 single-shot rifle as a sort of mini male right of passage. He taught me how to properly clean it, how to shoot it, and how to carry it in the field. This education started early in those days. Both my brother Will and I had owned Red Ryder BB guns for years. They were the firearms equivalent of training wheels. We were taught never to point a gun, even an unloaded one, at another person, and to never climb over a fence with a loaded gun. This was all folk wisdom passed down from people who had probably learned the hard way.

That summer, Will and I went on many shooting hikes out West Seventh Street. We put on our army web belts, filled our G.I. canteens with Kool-Aid, made ourselves peanut butter and jelly sandwiches, and headed for the wilds. We hiked down Second Street, crossed Highway 80, and went up Cemetery Road. When we got to the middle of Mountain View Cemetery, we loaded our rifles. Jackrabbits would sometimes be feeding on the fringe of the cemetery lawn; we wanted to be ready.

In those days, Seventh Street was just a winding dirt road that went less than a mile west of Keystone Avenue. An emergency dirt landing strip had been carved out of the sagebrush, but was abandoned after the war. There were many small dumping sites in the sagebrush, created by people too lazy to go to the dump across town. Will and I would set up bottles and cans for shooting practice, but we were always on the lookout for jackrabbits.

The month of August was my family's allotted time-share of the Clark family cabin at Lake Tahoe. The cabin had been built in the middle thirties by Grandmother Clark, my father, and Uncle David. It was a bare-bones summer cabin with no insulation, no screen doors or window screens, and the bathroom was a shed out back. The cabin was essentially one good-sized room with open truss roof, sleeping lofts at each end, and a native stone fireplace in the middle of the west wall. It was indoor camping.

Me and Betty with family dog Karen – Kings Beach, Tahoe

For us children it was heaven. Everyone wore bathing suits, T-shirts, and sneakers. Life was conducted in a back-to-nature mode. My grandmother had wisely leased two lots in the Cedar Flats summer cabin subdivision at eight dollars a year for ninety-nine years. This gave the cabin twice the land than most of the other cabins.

Tahoe in the forties had a quiet, national park ambiance. The roads were all narrow two-lanes. There was no gambling or nightlife. The lake itself was so clear that you could see the bottom in a hundred feet of water. Cedar Flats was about one hundred feet above the lake with a steep slope down to the water. Just below the cabin, the association had a hundred-foot stretch of beachfront with a dock that was available to lessees.

The Tahoe National Forest backed up to the cabin, offering unlimited space to play Davy Crockett and explorer. Will and I found a cross-country mile-and-a-half route through the forest to get to Carnelian Bay and the Tahoe Boat Company marina. We'd go there and drool over the speedboats.

The speedboats were magnificent—gleaming deep mahogany with chrome accents and magic names like *Chris-Craft, Gar Wood,* and *Century.* They were the height of glamour and excitement and the icons of the up-scale side of Tahoe. The lakeshore was populated by the rich and famous, while the backwoods had summer cabins of the middle class, making a two-tiered society.

We kids had a wonderful time. We tried to catch chipmunks, played ping-pong, went swimming at King's Beach or Carnelian Beach, and didn't have to wear school clothes, comb our hair, clean our rooms, or even wear socks. We were a family of little bear cubs frolicking in the forest sun.

September meant getting back to civilization—school clothes, school supplies, and a new school year. I was stoked. I was finally on the big kids' side with all the new sports possibilities—basketball, baseball, high bars, rings, and the horizontal ladder. My newfound skill at marbles was put to good use, but there was a downside to our return that fall. Over the summer, the school board had erected a ten-foot chain-link fence around the whole play yard. We were outraged. We were no longer trusted. We were once free-range children; now we had become caged animals. This was frequently discussed at lunchtime, but deep down we knew there was no appeal. The system had us.

Soon the leaves were turning, the mornings were crisp, and Thanksgiving was upon us again. My grandmother Clark was determined to have Thanksgiving at her house. It was to include the whole Clark family, with the Santinis and the Chisms. It turned out to be a social success with all having a great time. The only disappointment was Grandmother Clark's cooking. She had never cooked a meal until she was over fifty and you could tell she wasn't a natural. The turkey was dry, over-cooked, and tough. The stuffing, usually a favorite of mine, had the taste and consistency of sawdust, but the conversation and good cheer made up for it.

As the year was winding down, there was talk around our house that we were going to spend Christmas vacation camping in Death Valley. This didn't mean much to me. I was not a geography buff, tending to think of the world only in terms of a loose triangle between Pyramid Lake, Lake Tahoe, and Virginia City.

The expedition was to include the Craig Sheppard, Gus Bundy, and John Chism families. We assembled our war surplus tents and folding cots, got our camping stove cleaned up, and waited for Christmas vacation to start. There was snow on the ground and ice on the ponds when we headed east, then south, in a caravan of stuffed station wagons.

Death Valley was like the back of the moon. I thought that Pyramid Lake was as desolate as places got, but Death Valley was a whole new experience. As we descended into the valley, the scrub vegetation kept thinning until there was none. The temperature kept climbing until it reached Reno's summertime norms.

We made camp just above the valley floor, three hundred feet below sea level. It was not only summertime temperature, but we could run and run and never get tired. We felt like super kids. The moon was full during our stay so we could walk around at night as if it were twilight. The moon shone on the light-colored sand hills creating an eerie glow that lasted all night. There were only a couple of other camping groups in our area so we had the place practically to ourselves.

Christmas Day came. We exchanged small presents, but we didn't feel Christmassy at all. We just wanted to keep on exploring our newfound moonscape. We climbed cliffs, followed ancient dry streambeds, and hunted for geodes. We went on day trips to Scotty's Castle, Devil's Golf Course, and a wonderful set of sand dunes that stretched for miles. The sand dunes gave us the feeling that Arabs on camels were going to burst onto the scene at any moment. Time flew by. As we packed up and headed for home, we all felt like seasoned explorers. It was a good time.

EARLY IN THE NEW YEAR OF 1950, UNCLE DAVID stopped by our house and said that Washoe Lake was frozen over and a skating party was in order. We all were excited. The day was on the breezy and cold side, but the skating soon had us warm again.

The first ten yards offshore were impossible. The ice had broken up and then froze again, making a jagged uneven ice unsuitable for skating. We had to walk on it in our skates and most everyone fell in the attempt, but once over the fringe, the ice was fantastic. Literally miles of perfect, unblemished ice lay before us. This was a real treat. The ice on the ponds at Idlewild Park was so scarred and rutted that our skates chattered over the surface. The city fire department flooded the ponds at night, which improved the surface, but did not perfect it. That day, on Washoe Lake, the ice was perfect.

The wind was from the south. We had to put our heads down and battle our way from Little Washoe into

Big Washoe Lake. Just as we were about to drop from the effort, we turned around, opened our jackets to act as sails, and rocketed back north again. It was the sensation of flying in a dream. Effortless speed in crisp winter air on virgin ice—an intoxicating day.

About this time we got our first television set. To start with, the rules were strict. My mother was determined to save our young impressionable minds from this corrupting influence. The former upstairs playroom was now a finished TV room, as my mother vowed that there would never be a TV in our living room. We watched TV only in the evenings after dinner. It was strange. We were so attached to the radio that it was hard to make the switch. Everyone had his own idea of how Marshal Matt Dillon should look, but there he was on TV—not that it was better or worse, it was more the theater of the mind versus a given reality. I was initially disappointed.

We were excited to at last be part of the American mainstream, but television wasn't all that great. The programs weren't the big-budget, slick productions we have today. The television industry was in its infancy and was at war with the well-established radio and movie companies. The best programs seemed to be the variety shows with Jack Benny, Sid Caesar, and Bob Hope. *Playhouse 90* did some fine serious drama and the sports were good. Being kids we would watch anything my mother would let us.

The broadcasting towers were on local mountaintops. We had three channels and, for the first year, only rabbit ears for reception. Rabbit ears have since fallen into disuse, but in 1950, manipulating the two little antennas could attain fair reception. When a person had hold of the antennas the reception could be very good, but as soon as they let go, the ghosts and fuzz would return. There were terse exchanges before the position of the rabbit ears was agreed upon.

Betty was now twelve and on the brink of becoming a lady. This necessitated a reshuffling of our household. Betty was given the eastern upstairs bedroom with the new bath. The basement was paneled and a boys' dormitory set up. On the surface, it would seem an unfair arrangement, but somehow we knew mysterious forces were being played out.

As a family, eating out was usually limited to long car trips when we would occasionally stop at roadside restaurants. But an exception was made about every other month when the whole family went to the Chinese Pagoda for dinner. This was an exotic treat for us kids and the only restaurant my parents could afford.

The Chinese Pagoda was located in Sparks in the last commercial building on the east end of C Street at the corner of Stanford Way. It was a turn-of-the-century, two-story brick job about twenty by sixty feet. When we arrived it was usually dusk, which added to the mystery. The entrance was dark, with the bar to the left and the restaurant in the back. The decor was all gold dragons, lanterns, and dark red accents. Between the end of the bar and the beginning of the restaurant, a beaded curtain partially concealed a smoke-filled little room with half a dozen gentlemen playing Mahjong and excitedly speaking Chinese. It was a film noir setting. I loved the food and felt I had been in on some foreign intrigue.

In those days, Sparks was a separate town from Reno. Even though the commercial build-up between the two towns was pretty solid on Fourth Street/Highway 80, there was open farmland just off the highway, so dinner out was also a trip to another town. As we entered Sparks from Reno on C Street, everything to the right was the Southern Pacific maintenance shops (where the Nugget casino is today).

The Southern Pacific workshops were the reason for Spark's existence. The steam engines needed two hours of maintenance for every hour of running time, and the crossing of the Sierra mountains was the line's roughest test. Everything about the shops was dark and massive. In the middle there was a large classic engine roundhouse with a long turntable. Being a model train enthusiast, I loved it all.

The Korean War had started and there was adult talk of coming shortages, as there had been during the Second World War. Everyone was sure that they wouldn't be able to buy tires, construction materials, or desired food items, but that never happened. The Korean War was a messy abstraction that no one wanted. There wasn't any out-pouring of patriotism, no parades, and no shortages. It was a strange police action on the other side of the world.

New cars were the national obsession. The cars of the late forties were actually early forties cars rushed back into production. Now in 1950, the new post-war cars were in the dealerships. It is a little difficult now to understand how exciting the new cars were back then. We felt that we—America—had won the war and the new cars were America's expression of our new place in the world. They were bigger, more powerful, and had a strut-your-stuff attitude with a spaceship overlay—a sort of present to ourselves for all our sacrifices during the war. When a new car was introduced, there would be standing room only at that dealership for a week.

South Virginia Street was automobile row. The first couple of blocks had most of the new car dealerships, while the used car lots were found in the next mile. Johnson Chevrolet was at the southwest corner of South Virginia and Court streets, across from the courthouse. Their used car lot was at the corner, with their new car showrooms just to the south. The showroom could barely hold two cars.

Up the street to the south on Virginia was Scott Motors, the Cadillac and Buick dealer. Their showroom held only one car. Winkle Pontiac was on Ryland, a half block down from Virginia. The Ford dealer, Richardson and Lovelock, was not on the row, but instead was located on Fourth and Lake streets. All the dealerships were built in the twenties and thirties, proving to be cramped quarters as the postwar boom in take-home wages increased demand. Now that I had my bicycle, I could check the action out on my own.

Back at Chism's Auto Camp, we were adding more trailer spaces in the area that was formerly the clothes-drying yard and camping area. We would hand dig a trench about two feet deep through the middle of the proposed new spaces, then lay the water and sewer pipe. My father was the pick-man and I shoveled out the dirt.

When it came to installing the water pipe, my father was the in-trench guy. I cut and threaded the pipe to his order and he would assemble the pieces in the trench. It was three-quarter-inch galvanized water pipe and it took all I had to cut the threads. We had a sawhorse-type stand with a pipe vise on it. With a length of pipe secured, I would put the threader on the pipe end, get it started, douse the pipe and threader with cutting oil, and then work the ratchet handle up and down until the threads were cut. This required me to leap up in the air and put all my weight on the very end of the handle.

On a sunny afternoon, my father was down in the trench and I was doing my jumping-jack-thread-the-pipe routine, when a four-porthole Buick pulled up with four suits in it. My father got out of the trench and started talking to the men. I didn't know what to make of it as I listened on the sidelines. It seems that the suits in the power car had come to ask my father what they should do about a city government issue. This was a new dimension of my father. There he was in his T-shirt and Levi's giving advice to the powers that be. I was impressed and, of course, proud.

Now that my brother David was five, we could all go on trips together. My mother decided that taking us to San Francisco to see the Ice Follies would help us stretch and grow. Highway 80 was two-lanes all the way to the Bay Area and unbelievably curvy through the mountains. The frustration of being stuck behind a truck or bus going up a curvy grade at less than twenty miles an hour was a form of torture. The highway also went down the main streets of every little town on the route. We went through Truckee, Auburn, Loomis, Rocklin, Roseville, Sacramento, Davis, Vacaville, and Vallejo—stoplights, crosswalks, and all.

Cries of *are we there yet?* could be heard by the time we hit Sacramento, but once we got to the Golden Gate Bridge, our spirits picked up again. What a wonderful way to enter the city. The bridge, the ocean, and the city of hills combined to reveal a breathtaking vista for a station wagon full of kids from a high desert town.

We were booked at the Ocean View Motel across the street from the entrance to the San Francisco Zoo and about one hundred yards from the beach. The Ocean View Motel had a thirties nautical theme. The white stucco exterior had porthole windows, ship's railings, and even funnels on the flat roof. We thought it was great.

As soon as we checked into our room, all of us kids begged to go to the beach. The ocean, the big waves, the moist exotic smell, and the seemingly endless beach fascinated us. We collected sand dollars and shells and were soon racing the wave surges. Before long we were all wet up to our waists and had tasted salt water.

When we got back to the motel, our Levi's were soaked. We changed into our good pants believing we would be back in our Levi's after a couple of hours of drying time. When we headed back home two days later, they were still too damp to wear. Being from

Reno, we had no experience with a moist climate. We had a wonderful time—the zoo, Golden Gate Park, the aquarium, the de Young Museum, streetcars, cable cars, and Fisherman's Wharf. We were hicks from the sticks loving the big city experience.

The Ice Follies was our first encounter with big live entertainment. We had on our best outfits and our seats were on the edge of the ice. The lights went down, the orchestra began to play, and spotlighted skaters streaked by us close enough to touch. We were thrilled by the beautiful girls, costumes, and skating we didn't know existed. The comedy team of Frick and Frack had us in stitches. All in all, it was a wonderful trip.

My best friend Tink and I had been watching the construction of the new Reno High School from his house. It was getting down to the finishing touches, as it had to be ready for students in less than a year. On the construction site, about fifty yards from Tink's house, a gigantic pile of empty cardboard boxes was forming and it got bigger every day. The boxes were about two-by-two-by-three feet. Our best guess was that they were the boxes that the student desks came in. There were thousands of them, making a pile fifteen feet high and about fifty feet in diameter.

Tink and I found that we could burrow our way into the center of the pile by knocking the bottoms out of boxes and creating a tunnel. Once we got well into the interior, we fashioned a cave about eight-by-eight-feet wide and five-feet tall. We were excited by our ingenuity and told Tink's mother that we were going to take our sleeping bags out and spend the night in our cave. Tink's mother would have none of it. *No*, it was simply *no*. We pleaded, moaned, and threw fits, but nothing would change her mind. We spent the rest of the day moping about and making our displeasure known.

I spent that night at Tink's house. We woke up early the next morning and dashed out to our box pile cavesite. We found nothing but a fire truck and a steaming pile of ashes. The boxes had been burned in the night. We were stunned. If we had had our way, we would have been in those ashes.

This was a shock to me. Up to that point I believed the world was a stable, benign, and supportive background for us to frolic in. Here was proof that the real world could wipe us out if we were not more careful. This was a wakeup call. I had a lot to rethink that sobering morning.

The new school year came around and I was an upper classman—the fifth grade. I was now an established marble power player and had shoeboxes full of marbles to prove it. The fifth grade school teacher was Miss Petitcord. I was in love. She was a vision of grace, beauty, and intelligence. I didn't have a chance. I just stared at her for the first weeks of school. I was aware that there was an awkward difference in age, but nothing could sober me up.

The math was becoming more challenging. I liked this because I was good at the subject, making up for my obvious shortcomings with the written word. I was also enjoying the freedom that my bicycle afforded me, so I was getting to know a larger part of town.

The winter of 1950 came early, with a good snow pack in the mountains by the beginning of November. Then just before Thanksgiving, a strong warming trend moved in with rain. The rain in the mountains melted the snow and the river began to swell. It was odd to see so much water in the Truckee River. The rain kept falling and soon the roar of the river could be heard from blocks away. Large tree trunks and assorted flotsam could be seen riding the swells as the river galloped by. Our kid's river sanctuary was under six feet of water and the rain kept falling.

Soon it was obvious that the riverbanks could no longer hold the increasing flow of water. A call for volunteers to sandbag the downtown area went out. The people in Chism's Auto Camp were nervous. The river was easily ten feet above normal and had engulfed the English Mill Ditch bordering the auto camp. The water was within three feet of the wheels of the trailers along the ditch.

After a couple of days of this, the river went over its banks, flooded the downtown area and all the farmland east of Reno. Luckily the bank on our side of the river was about two feet higher than Idlewild Park on the opposite side, allowing the water to spread out to the south. Plans were made to pull all the trailers back from the riverside of the auto camp, but the river crested and began to recede. Everyone breathed a collective sigh of relief.

The downtown businesses within two blocks of the river were flooded, in spite of all the sandbagging. The tree limbs and trunks that had been washed down the river caught on the bridges, forming beaver dams at each cross-street bridge. It took months to muck out the silt and get things back to normal.

On the bright side, our beloved Pyramid Lake got enough water to bring its surface level up about three vertical feet. Still, everyone was shaken. Nature had given us all a wake-up call. We were not as all-powerful as we believed ourselves to be.

Christmas was still part of the dig-out-the-muck after the flood and wasn't the lighthearted season of past years. We tried to put on a brave face as the rest of the year slid away.

As WE RETURNED FROM CHRISTMAS VACATION AND the start of 1951, the school was abuzz with news. We learned that next year we were not going to be sixth graders at McKinley Park School. With the opening of the new Reno High School, the entire school system was being realigned. Sixth grade was going to be in the intermediate schools.

We were to attend Central Intermediate School in the fall—the old Reno High School between Arlington and West streets above Fourth. We would never be the top class at our wonderful little school by the river. And yet we felt a sense of adventure. We would be off to the big-time and we knew we could handle it.

As spring settled in and summer vacation became the light at the end of our tunnel, an excitement spread among the upper-class boys. The city marble championships were about to start. I felt I had a good chance at winning the fifth grade at my school, but marbles is not unlike golf—one mistake and you're finished. On the day of our school's finals, a referee was in attendance. He scribed the official ring in the dirt and officiated over the matches. My luck held and I won the McKinley Park School fifth grade finals. The city championships were next—Saturday and Sunday of the following week at Saint Thomas Aquinas School at Second and Arlington. I couldn't sleep for two nights leading up to the contest.

I arrived early in a sleepless daze. My name was called. I met my opponent, a quiet and determined Indian boy. We went out into the play yard and were assigned a ring. I broke into a sweat. The ring was painted on the *paved* play yard. I had never played marbles on asphalt. I didn't even know that marbles could be played on asphalt. We had to lag to a line to see who shot first. My competitor put his marble within inches of the line. I tossed my marble toward the line. I thought it would never stop as it rolled four feet past the line. My opponent got on all fours and knocked seven marbles out in quick succession. That was a win—seven out of the thirteen marbles. I was living a bad dream.

The rules came to my rescue. The rules stated that opponents had to have a shot at winning. So thirteen marbles were put back in the ring and I was given my chance. I shot seven out without a mistake. I couldn't believe it. It was a form of divine intervention. When I won the second go-around, I was in shock. I couldn't miss. I won the next round and was crowned Fifth Grade Marble Champion of Reno. The Veterans of Foreign Wars gave me a silver medal and my picture was put in the Reno Evening Gazette. Wow! I didn't believe it, but it was true.

I floated into summer vacation on a cloud. I was marble champ and I was going to Central Intermediate School in the fall. It was the same school that both of my parents had attended, but as their high school.

Late that summer of '51, my father casually asked me if I would like to go to the sports car races being held in town. I had no idea what he was talking about. Sports car? My mind groped for images, but the only possibility that surfaced was a Jeep-like affair with a cubbyhole for golf clubs or possibly a gun rack for duck hunting.

My father explained, but I just couldn't correlate this new information with the adult world I had come to know. Adults built special automobiles for the pleasure of high-speed driving on public roads? There was to be a race for these cars around Virginia Lake and past the golf course? Impossible!

My father and I arrived the morning of the race and walked to the pit area. My father knew a Jaguar owner who was going to race that day. There were only a couple of local cars participating. Most of the cars and drivers were from San Francisco or Los Angeles. The pits, located on Plumas where the city tennis center is today, were buzzing with activity. It had all the romantic excitement of my beloved fighter-pilot mystique. Dashing young men in the company of exotic women were preparing to do battle in these beautiful, fast machines.

The course ran clockwise, starting in front of the pits, then continuing north on Plumas, right onto Country

Club Drive down to Virginia Lake, then around the Lake and south on Lakeside Drive to Moana Lane, right on Moana going west back to Plumas, then north again to complete a lap. In 1951, this was the southern end of town—a place of horse pastures, small ranches, and open fields.

When at last the races started, I watched with saucer-like eyes that only an eleven-year-old can generate. Thundering Cadillac Allards and moaning Jaguars vying for the lead, snaked through the hay-bale-lined streets bordering Virginia Lake. I could not have dreamed such magnificence. Excitement, speed, and beauty—it was all too wonderful!

My pubescent mind had so far not gathered a single clue that such a scene could exist. The Allards and the Jaguars were certainly the stars, but my heart was captured by the swarm of MGs that buzzed through the middle of the pack. That night I lay drugged—over-dosed on new sights, smells, sounds, and ideas. My spinning mind couldn't stop. That sleepless night, I vowed that I would one day race sports cars. I knew then that attaching my star to becoming a P-51 pilot had been a childish fantasy, but racing sports cars had content. Sports car racing was a solid worthwhile goal.

School was about to start and my perspective on life was changing from local neighborhood to a bigger world. I was the fifth grade city marble champ and ready to move on with my new self-confidence. It was time to step out of the nest and try my wings.

I CHOSE TO END THIS REMINISCENCE JUST BEFORE I was to enter Central Intermediate School in the fall of 1951. This was the last time in my life that I had a handle on the world. During my McKinley Park School days, I knew my territory, my family, my neighborhood, and my place in the scheme of things.

In that wonderful decade of my youth, I was blessed with loving and understanding parents, a sister and two brothers whom I loved and who loved me. Yes, there were family disagreements and sibling rivalries, but no physical fights or long-standing grudges.

I thrived with a river and open land to explore and a positive, caring community to support me. I can't remember a time when the doors of our house were locked. My parents left the keys in the family car so they would always know where they were. I can't remember anyone having been in a fight that ended in injury. We were all positive, open-minded, and naïve—it was a

wonderful time to be a child. As to my post-1951 life—
I believe it can best be explained by a line from the
movie, *Out of Africa*:

> *"When the ancient map-makers came to the edge of
> the known world, they would write—beyond here
> there be dragons."*

Made in the USA
Charleston, SC
26 January 2010